Discover Crayford

Discover
CRAYFORD
and
ERITH

A comprehensive guide to CRAYFORD, SLADE GREEN, ERITH, BELVEDERE, ABBEY WOOD & THAMESMEAD

by DARRELL SPURGEON

GREENWICH GUIDE-BOOKS

Copyright © Darrell Spurgeon 1994

All rights reserved. No part of this book may be copied or otherwise reproduced, stored in a retrieval system, or transmitted, in any form or by any means, electronic, mechanical, photocopying, recording or otherwise, without the prior permission of the author.

First published in Great Britain 1995 by
Greenwich Guide-Books,
72 Kidbrooke Grove, Blackheath, London SE3 0LG
(phone 0181-858 5831)

Other volumes in the same series by the same author:
Volume I, covering Woolwich, Plumstead, Shooters Hill,
East Wickham, Abbey Wood & Thamesmead
Volume II, covering Greenwich, Westcombe & Charlton
Volume III, covering Eltham, New Eltham, Mottingham,
Grove Park, Kidbrooke & Shooters Hill
Volume IV, covering Bexley, Bexleyheath, Welling,
Sidcup, Footscray & North Cray
In preparation: a revised and updated edition of Volume I,
covering Woolwich, Plumstead & Shooters Hill

Front cover photograph is the Beam Engine House at the Old Works,
Crossness Sewage Works (Sir Joseph Bazalgette, 1865)
gazetteer reference Belvedere 34

Printed in England by Biddles, Guildford

A catalogue record for this book is available from the British Library
ISBN 0 9515624 4 4

CONTENTS

Foreword   page 6

CRAYFORD
Introduction   9
Section 'A' (Town Centre & Wansunt)   15
Section 'B' (Barnehurst)   23
Section 'C' (Barnes Cray, The Saw Mills & Whitehill)   25
Section 'D' (Crayford Marshes)   27
Suggested Walks   30

SLADE GREEN   32

ERITH
Introduction   34
Section 'A' (Central & East Erith)   39
Section 'B' (Lesney Park)   42
Section 'C' (West Erith)   44
Section 'D' (Northumberland Heath)   50
Suggested Walks   52

BELVEDERE
Section 'A' (Lower Belvedere)   55
Section 'B' (Upper Belvedere)   56
Section 'C' (Riverside Industrial Zone)   61
Suggested Walks   65

ABBEY WOOD
Introduction   67
Section 'A' (Lesnes Abbey & Woods)   69
Section 'B' (Lower Abbey Wood)   72
Section 'C' (Bostall)   73

THAMESMEAD
Introduction   77
Section 'A' (Thamesmead Central)   81
Section 'B' (Thamesmead North)   84
Section 'C' (Thamesmead South)   87
Section 'D' (Thamesmead West)   89
Suggested Walks   91

Bibliography   93
Index   94

MAPS
Crayford Sections 'A', 'B' & 'C'   14
Crayford Section 'D' & Slade Green   28
Erith general map   38
Belvedere Sections 'A' & 'B'   54
Belvedere general map & Section 'C'   60
Abbey Wood general map   68
Thamesmead general map & Section 'C'   76
Thamesmead Sections 'A' & 'B'   80
Thamesmead Section 'D'   90

FOREWORD

For each of the six areas covered by this guide - Crayford, Slade Green, Erith, Belvedere, Abbey Wood and Thamesmead - there is a basic framework consisting of brief introduction, gazetteer, map(s) and (except in the case of Slade Green and Abbey Wood) suggested walk(s).

This volume overlaps with the sections on Abbey Wood and Thamesmead in the first book of this series, 'Discover Woolwich and its Environs'; it is hoped this will not be considered an unnecessary duplication. In fact, some of the entries have been updated, and new locations have been included.

The areas covered by this book are in the London Borough of Bexley, except for: the areas in Abbey Wood and Thamesmead to the west of Brampton Road, Knee Hill, Harrow Manorway, and a line extending due north of Harrow Manorway, which are in the London Borough of Greenwich; and Wansunt Pit and the southern end of Station Road, Crayford, which are in Dartford Borough, and therefore in Kent not London.

From 1894 to 1920 Crayford and Slade Green formed part of Dartford Rural District, and from 1920 to 1965 constituted Crayford Urban District. From 1894 to 1938 Erith, Belvedere and the parts of Abbey Wood and Thamesmead now in Bexley Borough constituted Erith Urban District, and from 1938 to 1965 Erith Borough.

Each area has one or more maps and a detailed gazetteer. Every location in the gazetteer is identified (using location numbers) on a map. There are also suggested walks, but only where places of interest are concentrated within an area which makes walking practicable and interesting. The walks would be best followed in conjunction with the gazetteers and maps; the gazetteers indicate what to see at each location, and the maps make the route of the walks easier to follow.

Crayford is divided into four sections - Section 'A' Town Centre & Wansunt; Section 'B' Barnehurst; Section 'C' Barnes Cray, The Saw Mills & Whitehill; and Section 'D' Crayford Marshes. The introduction also covers Slade Green. There are two maps - one covering the first three sections, and one covering Section 'D' and Slade Green. There are suggested walks which cover most locations in Crayford Town, Barnehurst and Barnes Cray; the gazetteer entries for Crayford Marshes describe the walk around the Marshes along the banks of the Rivers Cray, Darent and Thames.

Erith is divided into four sections - Section 'A' Central & East Erith; Section 'B' Lesney Park; Section 'C' West Erith; and Section 'D' Northumberland Heath. One map covers all sections. The suggested walks cover most locations in Section 'A', 'B' and 'C'; there is no walk for Section 'D', as the locations are mostly near each other, and there is no need to suggest a route. The introduction to Erith is extended to cover Belvedere.

Belvedere is divided into three sections - Section 'A' Lower Belvedere; Section 'B' Upper Belvedere; and Section 'C' Riverside Industrial Zone. There are two maps - one covering Belvedere in general and Section 'C' in particular, and one covering Sections

FOREWORD - 7

'A' and 'B'. The suggested walks cover most locations in Lower and Upper Belvedere; the gazetteer entries for the Riverside Industrial Zone describe the riverside walk.

Abbey Wood is divided into three sections - Section 'A' Lesnes Abbey & Woods; Section 'B' Lower Abbey Wood; and Section 'C' Bostall. There is one map covering all sections. There are no suggested walks as the locations are either thinly spread over a large area or very closely concentrated; however, the gazetteer entries for Section 'A' describe a route through the Abbey ruins and contain advice on a walk through the Woods.

Thamesmead is divided into four sections, corresponding to the four officially designated residential zones. There are three maps - one covering Thamesmead in general and Thamesmead South in particular, one covering Thamesmead Central and North, and one covering Thamesmead West. The suggested walks cover most locations in Thamesmead Central and North; there are no suggested walks for Thamesmead South, where the locations are thinly spread over a large area, nor for Thamesmead West, where the locations are not numerous and are mostly near each other, and there is no need to suggest a route.

Although the introductions to the areas contain some historical background, and certain locations have some historical information in indented paragraphs, the guide is not a history of Crayford and Erith; it makes no pretensions to be a work of local history. Again, although some non-specialist knowledge of architecture is assumed, the guide does not become involved in detailed architectural analysis and a conscious attempt has been made to avoid architectural jargon. Readers interested in further information on local history and architectural detail may like to consult the list of books at the end of the guide.

The gazetteers are intended as a comprehensive list of buildings and landscape features which are of visual interest, though the choice of places is inevitably very personal. The emphasis is on what is there now, not so much on what has been there in the past, and practical information is given on how best to see each place.

The maps, which are the key to the guide, adopt the same practical approach. Virtually every place mentioned in the text is pinpointed on a map in such a way as to make it easy to find and notice. The maps are indicative and not to scale, and only show those roads which are likely to be important to the visitor. It is suggested that a more detailed road map of the area also be obtained.

The starring system in the gazetteers enables visitors to allocate their time to the best advantage. All locations which are starred are, in my opinion, worth a very special effort to see. Two stars are given to locations of outstanding importance, and one star to locations of particular interest. Most locations however are not starred, but they are still in my view worth seeing; such places invariably have interesting features and help to make the area distinct.

Italics are used for information on access, for other practical advice, for introductory notes before the walks, and also for cross-referencing. Paragraphs with information of a specifically historical nature are indented.

The sequence of locations in the gazetteers generally follows the order in the suggested walks, and locations not included in the walks are slotted into the sequence in a way which would make a visit most convenient to make.

Some locations are difficult of access, and the guide gives practical information on how to overcome this difficulty. In some cases this may not always be possible, but it is certainly worth trying. In other cases, a certain initiative is demanded; for example, it is usually necessary to phone or call at the clergyman's residence to obtain access to church interiors. In my experience most clergymen are extremely helpful in facilitating this. And many places which are private will not in practice turn away the interested visitor asking permission to view. The text includes contact telephone numbers and/or addresses which may be found helpful in this context.

Of the publications which I have consulted, I wish to make particular mention of: the section on Bexley, which is by John Newman, in 'London 2: South', by Bridget Cherry and Nikolaus Pevsner, in the Penguin Buildings of England series; the Department of National Heritage List of Buildings of Architectural & Historic Interest, which can be consulted at the National Monuments Record (London office), 55 Blandford Road, London W1; the survey of buildings carried out by the Bexley Civic Society in the 1970s and early 1980s; and a whole series of informative publications by Bexley Libraries and Museums. These and other publications which I have found useful are listed in the bibliography at the end.

I also wish to give very special thanks and acknowledgment to many local people who helped me in various ways. The staff at the Bexley Local Studies Centre at Hall Place - Malcolm Barr-Hamilton, Len Reilly, Frances Sweeny, Jessica Vale - dealt courteously and efficiently with my many requests for information, some of which involved much painstaking work; Malcolm Barr-Hamilton and Len Reilly also read the whole text and gave me much valuable advice. Michael Dunmow read the whole text, with particular reference to 'industrial archaeology' entries, and made a number of useful suggestions. Ted Thomas read my text on Crayford and Slade Green, John Prichard my text on Erith and Belvedere, and Willie Bossert (of Thamesmead Town) my text on Thamesmead; all made important comments which influenced my whole approach to certain sections of the guide. Also very helpful were Jim Packer, with information on pubs; Martyn Nichols and John Davison, of the Bexley Planning Department; Janet Hearn, at the David Evans works; Brian Sturt, with information on the gas industry; and Melanie Lorien, of the Bexley Rangers, with information on Lesnes Abbey Woods and Frank's Park.

Clergymen at all the churches were helpful in facilitating my visits, but I would wish to make particular mention of the ministers at Christ Church Erith, St Augustines Slade Green, and St Benets Abbey Wood. At St Johns Erith, Bob Knight and Peter Green gave me a lot of knowledgeable guidance.

Many thanks also to Jim Pope for invaluable advice and help with production, and Dave Belle (of Anchor Displays, Eltham) for expert processing of the photographs.

The area covered by this guide, like any urban area, is subject to the process of change, and the situation with regard to the condition and function (or even the existence) of buildings, their interiors, their accessibility etc can change quite rapidly. However, the information was checked before going to print, and if anyone is misled in any way, I can only offer my apologies.

Darrell Spurgeon,
Blackheath, December 1994

CRAYFORD

Introduction

Crayford is a town of outstanding historical and industrial interest, but this is difficult to imagine as one proceeds through on the main road between Bexleyheath and Dartford.

The impression one has now is of minor shopping parades, dominated by the new road system of 1986 around the large Sainsburys store and the new greyhound stadium. But opposite are vast industrial premises, giving an indication of Crayford's past as an important industrial town.

The historic centre is on a hill to the north, linked by the old High Street; it has an old church, a manor house, and several old buildings, all in a setting which remains quite rural and is full of character.

The area of Crayford covered by the gazetteers which follow includes Barnehurst, Barnes Cray and the Marshes. This introduction is extended to cover the area of Slade Green, which was once part of Crayford parish and Urban District Council.

Prehistoric Crayford

Flint implements from the Old Stone Age have been discovered at Wansunt Pit and at Bowmans Lodge, both on the edge of Dartford Heath overlooking Crayford from the south; they have been estimated to be about 200,000 years old. Also, a workshop of flint implements, probably between 50,000 and 10,000 BC, was discovered by the pioneering archaeologist Flaxman Spurrell at Stonehams Pit, off Perry Street, in the 1880s.

Also at Wansunt Pit, some remarkable late Bronze Age (about 1000 BC) discoveries were made in this century - 17 gold armlets in 1906-07, and a collection of axes in 1930. This may indicate a Bronze Age settlement in the area.

So there have been lots of prehistoric finds (all now in the British Museum), but the earliest settlement of which there is actual evidence is from the Iron Age, probably between 30 BC and 40 AD. The settlement was around St Paulinus Church, and was discovered in excavations on Old Road just to the west of the church in 1936, and on Iron Mill Lane to the east of the church in 1993. Some pottery finds are at Hall Place, and two iron knives at Dartford Museum.

The Romans at Crayford

It is now considered highly probable that the Roman military station of Noviomagus was in the area where Watling Street forded the River Cray at Crayford. Many Roman finds, including some building foundations, have been made in the vicinity; probably the most interesting was near Wallhouse Farm at Slade Green in 1957, when a group of Roman cremations and over 20 pottery vessels were uncovered.

There is disagreement amongst experts about the exact route of Watling Street, the Roman road from London to Canterbury and Dover. The most commonly accepted view is that it followed roughly the route of the A207 from Shooters Hill through Welling and Bexleyheath, then left this route to go along Old Road and along the back of the houses on the south side of Crayford High Street before rejoining the route at Crayford Bridge.

There is an alternative view that Watling Street followed the route of the A207 throughout, along London Road to Crayford Bridge; and that in the medieval period there was a diversion up Old Road, then down Crayford High Street to Crayford Bridge, which became the main road through Crayford until London Road was improved in the early 19th century.

From Crayford Bridge, Watling Street certainly followed roughly the route of Crayford Road on the way to Dartford.

The Saxons and the Normans

In the Saxon period Hengist defeated the Ancient Britons at the Battle of Crayford c457 AD. Faesten Dyke, the defensive linear earthwork of which sections have survived in Joydens Wood, was probably created by Hengist after this battle.

Later a Saxon church was built, on a hilltop site 35 metres above sea level, with commanding views to the south and east. The Saxon church was replaced, probably on the same site, by the Normans c1100, and the area around became a village which developed over the centuries down the hill of the High Street towards the river, with Bexley Lane cutting into the middle.

Industrial Crayford

Industry started on the eastern outskirts of the village in the 16th century, with an iron mill by the River Cray; there may have been a corn mill even earlier, and there was certainly a corn mill by the 17th century. The iron mill was replaced by a saw mill in the 1760s, and the area became known as The Saw Mills.

Fields by the River Cray began to be used for calico bleaching in the late 17th century. By the mid 18th century this had led to several textile printing works being set up by the river, mainly on the western side of the village.

In the 19th century textile printing and brickmaking were the main activities, but it was the arrival of Sir Hiram Maxim and his machine gun factory in 1888 which began to transform Crayford into an important industrial town. In 1897 the Maxim firm was taken over by Vickers, and engineering, particularly of armaments, but also of aircraft, motorcars and many other products, became the dominant industrial activity, leading to an enormous increase in the population.

Three key centres of industrial Crayford can now be determined: the area around the junction of Bourne Road and London Road, where textile printing still survives; the great industrial estates to the north of Crayford Road, which was the Vickers site; and The Saw Mills, where it all began.

The Saw Mills

In the 16th century an iron mill was set up at the end of Iron Mill Lane, which led from the church to a point on the River Cray. The site became an important industrial area; it is now marked by Crayford Flour Mill, at the head of Crayford Creek where the river becomes tidal. Thames Road, the main road which now isolates the site from the main part of Crayford, was not constructed until 1932.

A corn mill was set up by the 17th century, on a site adjacent to the iron mill. In the 1760s the iron mill was replaced by a saw mill, and the area became an industrial hamlet known as The Saw Mills. Both corn mill and saw mill had their own waterwheel. Warehouses and finishing shops connected with textile printing firms to the west of Crayford were also established there in the 19th century. Bricks, chemicals and carpets were other main products in the area, and barges were constructed on the Creek up to the 1920s.

Two terraces of mid 19th century housing built for workers in the area have survived.

The industrial estates

Three estates - the Rich Industrial Estate, the Crayford Industrial Estate to its rear, and the Acorn Industrial Park to its east - stretch for half a kilometre to the north of the main road through Crayford, between Crayford Bridge and the railway line. This was the heart of Crayford's industrial history, and it is still at the very centre of Crayford.

The estates now have a variety of users, but from 1888 until the 1970s it was the site initially of the Maxim Gun Company and then the firm of Vickers. Production began with the Maxim machine gun, and the site concentrated on machine gun and other munitions at wartime periods (including aircraft from 1914 to 1919), but switched to peacetime products at other times, the most notable being the Wolseley Siddeley motorcar from 1903 to 1910. During the first world war Vickers built housing estates, a coach station and a theatre, as well as a canteen and mess-room which became Crayford Town Hall in 1929.

Before the arrival of Maxim, the western part of the site was in large part devoted to the silk and calico printing works of Charles Swaisland. This was set up in 1824; the site was sold partly to Maxim and partly (in 1893) to G. P. & J. Baker, who continued textile printing until 1963.

Textile printing

The sole surviving textile printing firm in the London area is David Evans, whose premises are in the Bourne Industrial Park at the junction of Bourne Road and London Road. They are among the leading silk printers in Europe, and their history goes back to 1826, when Augustus Applegath set up his works (which pioneered new techniques in textile printing) on both sides of Bourne Road. In 1843 the business was acquired by David Evans, and in 1936 the firm consolidated on a site just to the south between a channel of the River Cray and the river itself.

In the mid 19th century housing for textile workers was developed on the hillside leading up to the old village centre.

Other industrial sites

Industrial activity has taken place in many other sites in and around Crayford. Until the First World War brickworks (manufacturing mostly London stock bricks) covered vast areas northwards towards Slade Green and Erith, using the brickearth deposits of the area. There is a vast quarry in Wansunt, by Dartford Heath to the south of

Crayford; and in this area are two important water pumping stations. There was a tannery from c1900 to 1952 by the Cray south of the junction of Crayford Road and London Road. To the north the land around Crayford Ness was occupied c1890 to c1962 by Thames Ammunition Works, which became part of Vickers Armstrong.

The fields south of the river at Barnes Cray, an area named by the Barne family, have also been the scene of much minor industrial activity.

The Barne family

In 1745 the Barne family, who were cloth merchants, arrived at May Place, a mansion of 15th century origin to the north of Crayford. The grounds embraced Crayford Manor House, and May Place came to usurp its position as the home of the Lord of the Manor.

In 1903 a golf course was set up in the grounds, and May Place became the clubhouse. In 1938 Crayford UDC acquired the golf course and the Manor House (rebuilt by the Barne family c1768 and again c1816), which became a community centre in 1949. May Place was demolished after a fire in 1959, and the present clubhouse is on the site.

The May Place estate was vast, extending east to the River Cray, and for a kilometre to the north. This enabled the Barne family to implant their name on two places in the Crayford area - Barnes Cray to the east and Barnehurst to the north.

By 1800 they had given their name to Barnes Cray, an established hamlet on the river with a mansion and a farm. In the 19th century the fields to the south of the river were used for bleaching by the textile firms of Swaisland, Applegath and David Evans, and they became a minor industrial centre, with fabric printing, india-rubber manufacture and carpet production taking place there at different stages. During the first world war Vickers established workshops in the fields, and developed a large housing estate north of the river for its munitions workers.

In 1895 the Barne family gave their name to Barnehurst as a new railway station on the Bexleyheath Line. The expected housing development did not however get under way here until after the railway had been electrified in 1926. New Ideal Homesteads (who were the most prolific housing developers in the London area in the 1930s, with the greatest concentration of their estates in the general Bexley area) built the Barnehurst Park Estate to the north of the golf course in 1933.

Wansunt

Wansunt was an ancient settlement to the south of Crayford below Dartford Heath, and is the site of numerous prehistoric finds after quarrying for sand and gravel started there in the late 19th century. A railway station was located in this area with the arrival of the Dartford Loop Line in 1866. Station Road links the station with the Heath; development along the western side of Station Road had commenced even before 1866, and this side was fully built up as far as the Heath by the end of the century.

In this area there are ample natural supplies of water from underground springs. A water pumping station was constructed on the east side of Station Road in 1865, and another in a forested area by the railway line in 1901.

Slade Green & Howbury

A short distance to the north of the Saw Mills site is the railway town of Slade Green, originally part of the Norman manor of Howbury; the moat and moat walls of the original manor house are still there. The moated site, with the 17th century Howbury Tithe Barn nearby, is one of the most atmospheric and historically important in the Crayford area. The nearby Howbury Grange is on the site of a Saxon settlement.

The North Kent Line came through in 1849, and sidings were opened to brickworks to the west, but there was no station until 1900. Before that date the area remained quite rural, with just the Manor House, the Grange, a farm, a few cottages, two pubs and a school. The workers for the brickworks came mainly from the substantial hamlet of North End, on Northend Road; only Claremont Terrace of 1885 at the beginning of Peareswood Road survives from this hamlet.

The South Eastern Railway opened the station of Slades Green (as it was then called) in 1900 and a large maintenance depot in 1901, and the area was transformed quite quickly. An estate for railway workers, an electricity generating station, a parish church and the Railway Tavern were all built around the same time. Slade Green remained predominantly a railway town until the 1930s, when new housing estates appeared.

Slade Green still seems remote and isolated, sandwiched between the railway line and the marshes. After the railway came through, there had been no direct access by road until 1960, when Bridge Road was built over the railway; before that, the area could be accessed only by two level crossings and pedestrian bridges, at Slade Green Road and at Moat Lane.

Crayford Marshes

Slade Green is cut off from Dartford Creek (the tidal part of the River Darent) and the Thames to the east by the Crayford Marshes, which surround the area within a great semi-circle.

The southern part is a landfill site, but the northern part is the most important area of marshland, with drainage ditches and grazing pastures, surviving on the south bank of the Thames before reaching Dartford Creek. It is possible to walk right round the fringe of the Marshes, along the river wall of the Cray, Darent and Thames, from Crayford Flour Mill to the Erith Yacht Club. It is a walk of nearly three miles, but one passes the Dartford Creek Flood Barrier and the headland of Crayford Ness, a location of great atmosphere despite the rather unpleasant industrial activity behind.

Coal Duty boundary markers

In 1851 and 1861 London Coal and Wine Continuance Acts were passed enabling the City of London to set up boundary markers to demarcate the area within which they had the right to levy a duty on coal and wine brought into the metropolitan area, a right which existed from 1666 until 1889.

A number of such markers, all bearing the City of London shield, have survived in the Crayford area. They are mostly cast iron posts under the 1861 Act, which were erected at roadside locations; but two relatively rare markers of the 1851 Act have also survived - a tall granite obelisk by the railway line near Barnes Cray, and a small stubby granite pillar near the river on Crayford Marshes.

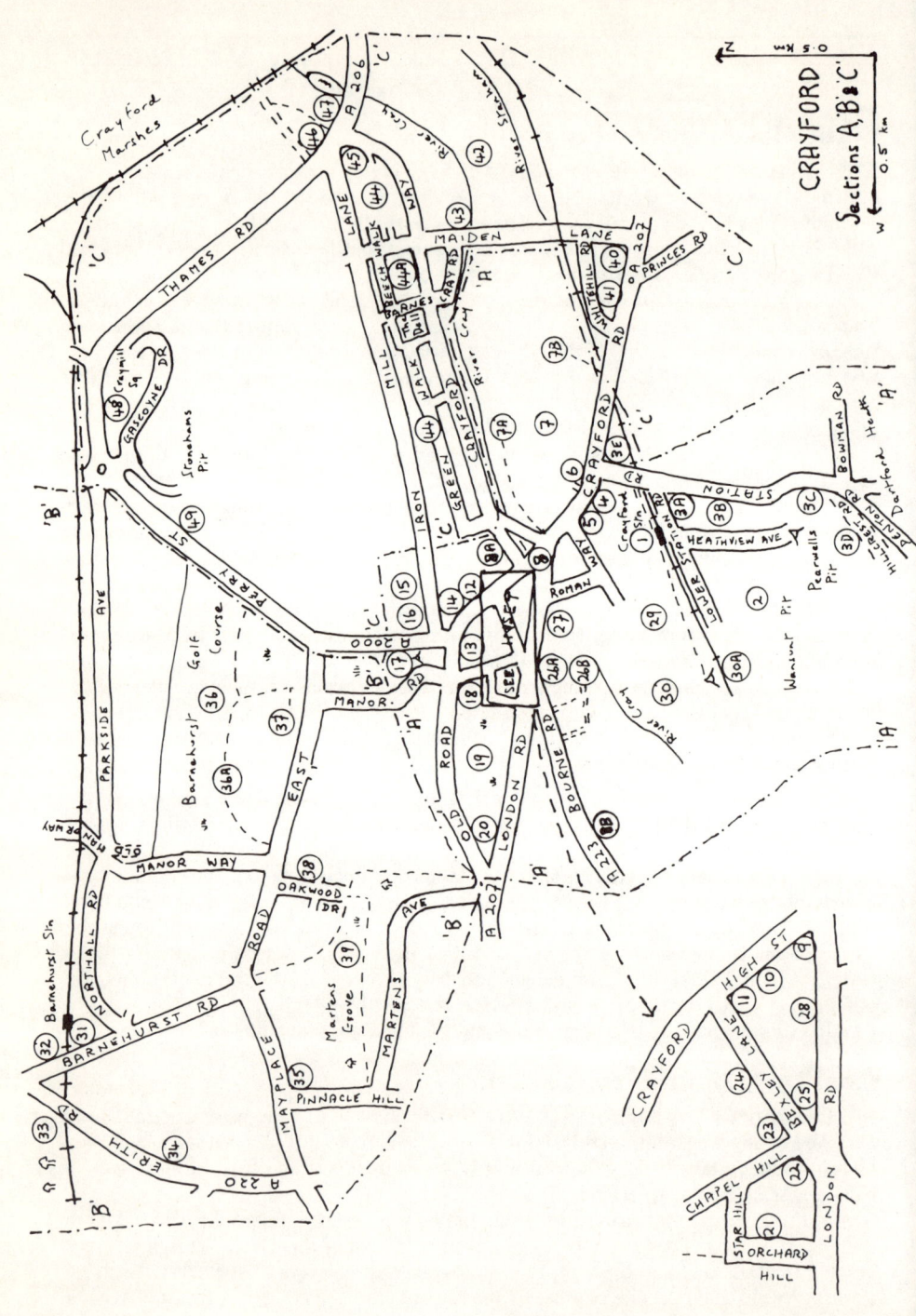

CRAYFORD

Gazetteer

Section 'A' TOWN CENTRE & WANSUNT

1. Crayford Station. First opened 1866, on the Dartford Loop Line. The present very basic building is of 1969.

2. Wansunt Pit. This vast quarry, also known as the Gun Club Quarry, is on the site of the ancient settlement of Wansunt. It has been an important site for prehistoric discoveries - Bronze Age finds here earlier this century, and Old Stone Age finds in the adjoining **Pearwells Pit** in the 1880s *(see introduction, page 9)*.

In the quarry, quite near the office portacabin, though almost hidden in the undergrowth, is a **coal duty boundary marker**, a cast iron pillar of 1861 *(see introduction, page 13)*.

There is no public access to the quarry site, but there is a good view of Pearwells Pit, an almost enclosed space with steep sided cliffs, at the end of Heathview Avenue. There is also a view, though not all that satisfactory, of the site as a whole by peering over the fence along Denton Road on Dartford Heath.

3. Station Road. This road leads from Crayford Road past the railway station up to Dartford Heath. Development started on the west side in the mid 19th century, even before the opening of the railway in 1866. Survivors of the early development are **The Royal Charlotte (3A)**, a pub of 1864, the terrace of cottages **nos 78/82**, and **no 88 (3B)**, with its classical portico. By the end of the century the western side was fully built up as far as the Heath.

At the top is a **coal duty boundary marker (3C)**, a cast iron pillar of 1861 *(see introduction, page 13)*.

Hillcrest Road leads off to the west. **Nos 1/2 (3D)**, formerly called Edith Villas, are an extraordinary pair, probably of the 1870s, with amazing decorative flourishes on the front.

Bowmans Road leads off to the east. To the south was the **Bowmans Lodge** sand and gravel pit, where Old Stone Age finds have been made.

At the lower end of the road is a modern Thames Water installation **(3E)** of 1960, replacing the original Waterworks Pumping Station of 1865.

4. Crayford Town Hall, Crayford Road. A handsome red brick classical building, with a long recessed portico. It was built by Vickers in 1915 as the canteen and mess room for workers at the factory opposite. It was purchased by Crayford Urban District Council in 1929 and used as the Town Hall until 1965, when the London Borough of Bexley was created.

5. Comet Store, Crayford Road. The frontage is modern, but the part behind is the old Vickers Coach Station, built by Vickers c1915 for coaches used for transporting their workers who lived further afield.

6. Clock Tower, Crayford Road. This quirky but pleasing red brick clock tower was built by Dartford Rural District Council in 1902. It served the dual function of acting as a sewage lift station and commemorating the coronation of Edward VII. It stands at the main entrance to the Rich Industrial Estate.

7. Rich Industrial Estate, with at the rear **Crayford Industrial Estate (7A)** and to the east (alongside the railway line) **Acorn Industrial Park (7B)**. A really vast industrial area, with some interesting older buildings remaining. It embraces both the former silk and calico printing works of Charles Swaisland, taken over and reduced in extent in 1893 by G. P. & J. Baker, and, occupying a much larger area, the former Vickers works. The Swaisland works was to the north and west alongside the river, and the Vickers works to the south and east.

Swaisland Drive leads straight ahead into the old Swaisland / Baker works, now occupied by the Crayford Industrial Estate. The only old buildings are a terrace of three mid 19th century cottages which may once have been Swaisland premises.

The main entrance into the Rich Industrial Estate is by the clock tower. This estate occupies the older part of the Vickers works. First one comes to some buildings from the period 1903-10 when Wolseley-Siddeley cars were produced here. Immediately to the left of the entrance is the finishing shop, and further on, slightly to the left, the chassis erecting shop (now partly covered by corrugated iron); across the lane to the right of this is a series of parallel adjoining buildings which were repair shops, engine shop, store-rooms etc. Continuing ahead, beyond a lane, one comes to buildings on both sides of the road which were part of the Maxim Nordenfeldt machine gun factory in the 1890s. Beyond this complex and to the right is a way into the Crayford Industrial Estate.

The Acorn Industrial Estate occupies the later part of the Vickers works. One can still see the vast grassed square which was surrounded on three sides by the main works of Vickers-Armstrong c1930, though the buildings themselves have been replaced by more modern ones.

> The Maxim Gun Company, which made Sir Hiram Maxim's machine guns, moved from Hatton Garden to Crayford in 1888 on part of the old Swaisland site. The same year it amalgamated with the Nordenfeldt Gun & Ammunition Co, which had opened in Erith in 1887, to form the Maxim Nordenfeldt Gun & Ammunition Co. In 1897 they were purchased by Vickers and became Vickers Son & Maxim Ltd. The site expanded, continuing the production of machine guns until the end of the Boer Wars.
>
> In 1903 the Crayford works started production of the Wolseley-Siddeley motorcar, but in 1910 this moved to Birmingham. In 1911 the name of the firm was changed to Vickers Ltd, and in 1912 it resumed munitions production. In 1914 it also began to manufacture aircraft, which were flown from Joyce Green Aerodrome on Dartford Marshes, the drainage ditches being covered by boards. Production increased enormously during the first world war, particularly of machine-guns, and Crayford became an important industrial town. At the peak of wartime production the Crayford works was employing 14,500 people. During the war Vickers built estates at Barnes Cray, Whitehill and Northumberland Heath to house its workers, and also built the canteen and mess room, now known as Crayford Town Hall, the old coach station (now Comet Store), and the Princesses Theatre (demolished 1957).
>
> Production of aircraft was transferred to Weybridge and Southampton in 1919, and the works turned to a variety of peacetime products. Motorcars were again made, as

Wolseley Motors, 1925-28. In 1927 Vickers amalgamated with Armstrongs to form Vickers Armstrong Ltd. and the manufacture of munitions resumed, particularly after the Erith works closed in 1931. During the second world war production was concentrated on machine guns and anti-aircraft fire control gear (especially for the Navy); over 10,000 persons were employed at the peak.

After the war armaments works continued until the Korean war, but by the mid-60s the Crayford works was concentrating on precision engineering, particularly fire-control equipment, boxmaking machinery, hardness-testing machines, and bottling machinery. But despite this diversification the presence of Vickers in Crayford began to decline, and came to an end in the 1980s. Crayford had been the main Vickers works in South East London. *(See also Erith 23.)*

8. Crayford Bridge. The brickwork on the north side of the bridge is of 1938, and incorporates two stone tablets, one with the date 1755 (when a former bridge was rebuilt by the New Cross Turnpike Trust), and the other with the date 1938. On the south side a stone tablet stating 'widened 1920' indicates the date of that side.

To the north of the bridge is Cray Gardens, a small green oasis with willow trees overhanging the River Cray, laid out in 1938. On the east side of the river is a defunct drinking fountain, inscribed to 'S. A. Blackwood in grateful remembrance of Christian work in Crayford 1871-80'. Stevenson Arthur Blackwood was an evangelist preacher; he resided at Crayford Manor House, and was the father of Algernon Blackwood *(see 37)*.

On the wall of 8/15 Waterside, the shopping parade to the left built 1961, is a stone reading: 'This stone was laid by HRH Princess Christian 1916' **(8A)**. It was from the **Princesses Theatre**, built by Vickers in 1916 on this site. The theatre was largely rebuilt in 1919 after fire damage; it became a cinema in 1921, and was demolished in 1957.

Two intricately decorated cast iron **lamp posts (8B)** of 1919 which were outside the theatre are now outside Bourne Road Garage, Bourne Road. They were made by Vickers at Barrow, but are now in a sadly truncated state; both lamps are missing, and one has the upper part of the post missing as well.

9. The Bear & Ragged Staff, occupying a key location looking down Crayford Road. There was a pub on the site at least by the late 17th century, but the present building is of 1925, with timber-framed bays jutting forward and many Tudor features.

10. 25/35 Crayford High Street. This is the oldest group of buildings in the shopping centre. Nos 31/33 are the central feature, and from across the road can be seen to be an 18th century house, though the windows of no 31 have been drastically altered and the shopfronts are modern; originally the entrance was from the rear, via Bexley Lane. Framing the older house, nos 25 & 27/29 and no 35 are probably basically early 19th century.

11. The Crayford Arms, Crayford High Street. A pleasing pub of 1864, recognisably formed from a group of cottages.

12. Grove Place, 90/100 Crayford High Street. A pair and a four-house terrace of 1841, forming an attractive group with a commanding position looking down the road.

18 - CRAYFORD

13. *The One Bell, Old Road. A very handsome pub, its present appearance of the early 19th century, though it may contain 18th century structure. It is imposing with its two-storey canted bays on either side of the central doorway, and a long swooping roof at the rear; note also the elaborate dentilled cornice across the first floor on top of the two bays.

Adjacent to the east are **172/6 Old Road**, formerly called The Limes, now in a state of extreme dereliction. The core of this group is considered to be a 17th century timber-framed house, but this is hidden by later additions. The group is at present difficult to see, as it is covered by scaffolding and netting.

14. 8a/20 Iron Mill Lane. This is a rather sombre Gothic group of 1865. The centre of the group forms a sort of square, consisting of no 10, **the Clergy House**, and nos 12/16, **Mrs Stables Almshouses**, forming two sides of the square (the extension projecting towards the road is of 1909). No 10 was originally built by the Swaisland family as a cottage hospital; Mrs Stable was the niece of Charles Swaisland.

On either side are other buildings of 1865 - to the east **nos 18/20**, and to the west **no 8a**, which was built as a public wash-house, but then became the rooms of the Young Mens Friendly Society.

15. St Paulinus School, Iron Mill Lane. The section to the left is of 1974, the section to the right of 1983. The earlier part includes a strange building with roofs sweeping down almost to ground level; the hall has a narrow elongated stained glass window.

16. Pims Almshouses, 7/13 Iron Mill Lane, an attractive composition of 1910 consisting of a long one-storey building attached to a more substantial two-storey building to the west. Mr Pim lived at Martens Grove *(see 39)*.

17. **Church of St Paulinus. This is the parish church of Crayford, an extraordinary church in that it consists of twin naves, with the chancel positioned at the end midway between them. It is largely early 14th century, of ragstone and flint, though much of the walling in the north nave is Norman; the tower and south chapel, which are both battlemented, the porch, and most of the windows were added in the 15th century. It occupies an elevated site with tremendous views to the south.

> There was a church in Crayford, probably on this site, in Saxon times. It was rebuilt c1100, and the original Norman church forms basically the north nave of today, but with the door at the west end. A south aisle was added c1200, with Norman windows and a Gothic door; at the same time a Gothic door was added in the north wall.
>
> In the early 14th century the south aisle was replaced by a second nave, roughly as wide as the existing one, and the old windows and door were repositioned in the south wall; a new chancel was built at the end midway between the two naves, a highly unusual phenomenon, occurring only at two other churches in England - Caythorpe, Lincolnshire, and Hannington, Northamptonshire.
>
> Additions of the 15th century included the tower, the present arcade, the south porch, a vestry and a chapel to the north of the chancel, and a chapel to the south of the chancel. Most of the windows were replaced in the 15th century, and these are the square-headed ones we see today.

Victorian restoration took place in 1862, but did not substantially alter the appearance of the church; the east window was reconstructed, but other windows, though restored, were not altered in shape. The south chapel was extended c1865. The north vestry was extended c1960.

Looking at the exterior, the tower is at the west end of the south nave. The west wall of the north nave is basically c1100; traces of the lower part of the blocked Norman doorway c1100 can be discerned below the 15th century window. At the north-west corner, amongst the stone quoins can be seen some blocks of tufa, a black chalk deposit often used in the Norman period.

The north wall is basically c1100, except for the last bay before the modern vestry, which is early 14th century. Traces of Norman windows c1200, rather high up, can be made out. The blocked doorway is early Gothic c1200.

At the east end, the chancel window is of 1862. To the right is the square-headed window of the 15th century vestry. The window in the south wall of the chancel is early 14th century.

In the south wall, between two square-headed 15th century windows, is one round-headed window c1200; it was repositioned here in the early 14th century, blocked in the 15th century, and opened up again in the late 19th century.

The **interior** is of great interest and has many fascinating features, in particular the position of the arcade, and the monuments to the Draper family and Elizabeth Shovel.

The church is normally open 0900 to 1200 Mondays to Saturdays; from 1200 to 1700 the room at the base of the tower is open, allowing a view of the interior. Otherwise contact the Rectory, Claremont Crescent, 01322 522078, or 1a Iron Mill Place, 01322 558789.

Entrance is through the 15th century south porch (note the conjectural drawings of stages in the church's history on the wall) and then through the early Gothic doorway of c1200. The font, near the entrance, is 15th century.

The dominant feature of the interior is the arcade, abutting the wall above the apex of the chancel arch; it is 15th century (note the fine shafts with hollows in between), and replaced an earlier arcade in this position. Traces of blocked windows c1200 are visible in the north wall, above the arch at the east end of the north nave, and also, repositioned of course, in the south wall.

The handsome pulpit is of 1630, which is also the date of the open timber roof. At the east end of the north nave is a 16th century parish chest; and above this can be seen the blocked entrance to the rood-loft stairs.

In the south wall of the chancel are the piscina and fragments of the sedilia, all 14th century. In the middle of the chancel is a painted altar-table, designed by James Brooks 1895; behind is the painted tryptich of an earlier reredos. Through a door in the north wall of the chancel is the 15th century vestry, and beyond the extension of c1960.

In the round-headed window in the south wall is a stained glass figure of St Paulinus of 1899; this, and stained glass of 1878 in a window in the east wall of the south chapel, are the only stained glass to have survived the war. Several windows have colourful modern stained glass by Hugh Easton 1955.

There are many fine monuments. The most outstanding is the Draper Monument of 1652 in the north chapel; it is a large monument of black and white marble, with striking figures of the wife lying above and behind the husband, two children kneeling, and right at the bottom, a still-born child in swaddling clothes.

Also outstanding is the large monument to Elizabeth Shovel (widow of Admiral Sir Cloudesley Shovel) 1732 in the south chapel; it has much elegant detail - note the canopy, the putti, the sarcophagus.

Other noteworthy monuments include: Blaunche Marlar c1600, with a kneeling figure, on the north wall of the chancel; Margaret Collins 1732, a cartouche with an inscription ending with an interesting verse, on the south wall of the chancel; Robert Mansel 1723, of grey-veined marble, in the south chapel; Henry Tucker 1851 (but in 17th century style), above the blocked north doorway; Elizabeth Barne (wife of Miles Barne) 1747, with nice classical details, at the east end of the north nave.

The **churchyard** (approached through a fine Gothic lychgate of 1873) is extensive, picturesque and crammed with tombs; it lies high above the road behind a brick and stone retaining wall. The most interesting tombstone is to Peter Isnell 1811, with a verse inscription of 13 lines, 6 ending with 'Amen' and the other seven rhyming with 'Amen'; it is now located against the wall of the south nave, under the round-headed window (it is mostly illegible, but the full text is in the guide-book on sale in the church, and also on the wall of the porch, though neither give an accurate indication of its present location). Note also, near the southern wall, the large table tomb 1874 to David Evans, the local textile printer, and family.

18. St Mary of the Crays Church, Old Road. A modern red brick Roman Catholic church of 1972 with a small campanile; it replaced a church built by Augustus Applegath in 1842. The interior is worth viewing *(contact the Parish Priest, 111 Old Road, phone 01322 523492)*, particularly for the altar, font, lectern and tabernacle, all of Cornish granite c1985.

Adjacent to the west is **St Josephs School**, mostly modern, but incorporating a small Gothic building, which was the original school building of 1866.

19. Shenstone Park. An attractive area of undulating parkland, with fine views to the south. It was formerly the grounds of the house called Shenstone *(see 26)*, which was built c1828 for Augustus Applegath, and occupied and enlarged by David Evans in the 1840s, remaining in the family ownership at least until 1935. It was demolished c1974, and Shenstone School is now on the site. The pattern of Shenstone Park is continued across London Road in Bigs Hill Wood.

20. Crayford Gas Works, London Road. The site was opened in 1852, and was acquired by the West Kent Gas Company in 1865, becoming known as the Nettle Bottom Works. The production works closed in 1912, and the site became a holder station. The brown column guided holder is of 1932, and the green spirally guided holder is of 1955.

> The West Kent Gas Company was established c1862, with gas works at West Street, Erith. The Crystal Palace & District Gas Company was formed in 1853, and became the South Suburban Gas Company in 1904; it took over the West Kent Company in 1912, and closed the Erith works c1914. *(See also Erith 27, Belvedere 2.)*

21. *Orchard Hill. This steep, narrow road with a surface of stones set in concrete has great character, with the tall trees of Shenstone Park on one side and terraced houses (built to house textile printing workers) on the other. The houses are of 1866-67, and the effect is most attractive - only no 5, which is modern, breaks the pattern.

Orchard Hill continues as a footpath up to Old Road. The steep neighbouring streets of **Chapel Hill** (built 1865-75) and **Star Hill** are similar in character, and together with the houses along the north side of London Road form a mid 19th century enclave. The north side of Star Hill is probably c1860, its pavement consisting of a series of steps.

22. Crayford Baptist Church, Bexley Lane. A handsome church of 1867, with an imposing classical frontage and round-headed windows along the sides.

Behind is the **Sunday School**, a smaller building of 1858 which had been an earlier Baptist chapel.

23. 56/64 Bexley Lane. This terrace comprises nos 56/62, early 19th century forming an imposing group with fine door-hoods, and no 64, late 18th century.

24. 38 Bexley Lane, formerly called Brooklands, an early 19th century house, handsome and well-proportioned, with a fine Doric doorcase.

25. The Duke of Wellington, London Road. A pleasing brick pub of 1853, with a canted projection to the west which was the original entrance.

26. Bourne Industrial Park, which incorporates the famous David Evans works, one of the leading silk printers in Europe and the sole survivor of the old London textile printers.

On the frontage to London Road is the **Long Shed (26A)**, with its pantiled roof, originally 18th century farm buildings; it was once an integral part of the David Evans factory, but is now largely in other use. (Note the Edward VII wall letter-box at the eastern end.)

To the west of the Long Shed is the red brick wall, partly 18th century, of Bexley House, an 18th century mansion demolished c1980. The site of the house is now occupied by **Crest House**, a pastiche c1982 of a Georgian mansion, though not in any way a replica of Bexley House; it is merely a facade to the industrial building behind.

To the rear of the Industrial Park is the ***David Evans works (26B)**, covering a large area, with the River Cray just beyond the boundary fence. There is a pleasant, now ornamental, stretch of water at the entrance to the site; this is part of a channel from the river, and was formerly lined by washing machines of the type which can be seen in the exhibition *(see below)*, which were used for washing silk after dyeing and printing. The works is mainly modern, developed from 1936 onwards, though one small building - known as the Madder Shop, probably c1840, with a pantiled roof - remains from the old works; it is situated near the entrance to the Craft Centre, and in front is an old piece of machinery which was a Gum Mixer.

The works incorporates the **Craft Centre of Silk**, an exhibition on the history of silk craftsmanship. The tour of the exhibition starts with a large montage of a dockside scene with a silk clipper, and an old washing machine still functioning *(see above)*, continues with a video on silk printing, then proceeds to a long table used for hand and carriage screen printing, a replica block-makers workshop, and a reconstruction of Victorian shop windows displaying silk products; there are also examples of old machinery and other artefacts.

The exhibition is open Mondays to Fridays 0930-1700, Saturdays 0930-1630. Admission charge. There is a coffee shop, and a silk craft shop. Groups visiting the works are shown other areas including the finishing shop; indiviuals wishing to take the full tour should ring 01322 559401 to see whether they could join a group tour.

Textile bleaching and printing in England first started in the London area from 1676; it was mainly calico and silk, and a location by a clear river like the Cray was important. It was not until after c1785 that London was outstripped by factories in Lancashire and in Scotland.

Textile printing did however survive in Crayford, and several factories, some quite large, were established in the 18th century. Charles Swaisland established his cotton printing works c1815 on the present Rich Estate, and used fields at Barnes Cray for bleaching The Swaisland business was taken over by G. P. & J. Baker in 1893; they also produced rugs and carpets, and continued until 1963.

In 1826 a site to the west of Crayford, at the junction of Bourne Road and London Road, was acquired by Augustus Applegath, who began to concentrate on silk and pioneered new techniques in paper as well as in textile printing. His works covered a large area on both sides of Bourne Road. He also used fields nearby and at Barnes Cray for bleaching, and had a warehouse and finishing shop at The Saw Mills. He built the house of Shenstone, the grounds of which are now Shenstone Park *(see 19)*, to the north of London Road.

In 1843 his business (as well as Shenstone) was acquired by David Evans, a City silk merchant. He was the founder of David Evans & Co, the sole survivor of the old London textile printers. In 1936 the firm moved its main buildings to the area across the channel of the River Cray, and the old site was gradually relinquished, now being occupied by the Bourne Industrial Park and by Beech Haven Court (on the other side of Bourne Road).

The firm has since 1979 been through several changes in ownership. It is now called David Evans, Vanners & Co Ltd, and is one of the leading quality silk printers in Europe, with over half its production being exported to North America.

27. Wolsley Close, a well-designed housing estate of 1980, with an ingenious variety of enclosed spaces.

28. 4/6 London Road. This group was originally the premises of the Crayford Friendly Funeral Society, built 1904, and seems an odd survival in this location. Behind are some industrial buildings which were part of the premises of Lyles Mineral Water Works, built 1902.

29. Crayford Greyhound Stadium, incorporating Crayside Leisure Centre, built 1986. The first greyhound stadium was built here in 1932.

30. Crayford Stadium Rough, a large area of roughland behind the Stadium, flat but wild and interesting, containing several wild plants rare in the London area. It is fringed to the north by the River Cray.

The area is not accessible from the Stadium, but is best approached by a footpath at the end of Station Approach, to the north of the railway line; this is continued by a path across the area which leads to the grassed open space to the east of Hall Place. At this point can be seen across the railway line the **Wansunt Pumping Station (30A)** of Thames Water, opened 1901.

CRAYFORD

Gazetteer

Section 'B' BARNEHURST
(See map on page 14)

31. Barnehurst Station. The station on the Bexleyheath Line was opened in 1895. The main station building, on the south (up) side, is brick, of 1932. Part of the original weatherboarded building can still be detected behind, and the iron footbridge is original too (in fact the only original one on the line).

32. The Red Barn, Barnehurst Road. This red brick pub of 1936, overlooking the railway station, contrasts with the mock-Tudor shopping centre around.
It provided the inspiration for the British postwar revival of New Orleans jazz, when George Webb's Dixielanders played here in 1944. This is commemorated by a plaque (unveiled in 1985) on an outside balcony overlooking the garden.

33. Bursted Wood. A large and pleasant open space, with a grassed area to the north and woodland (mainly sweet chestnut and oak) to the south.

34. Church of St Martin, Erith Road. This red brick church, the parish church of Barnehurst, was built in 1936. It is quite handsome, with its open bell turret, elongated windows, and a circular window over the brick porch.
The **interior** *(contact The Vicarage, 93 Pelham Road, phone 01322 523344)* is imposing, with great brick arched arcades, and a pure white sanctuary, added in 1972.

35. Sarahs Cottages, 74/80 Mayplace Road East. Two pairs of 1860, a surprising survival here. No 76 is the least altered house.

36. Barnehurst Golf Course. This was the heart of the old May Place Estate, and the **clubhouse (36A)**, a building c1960, occupies the site of the mansion of **May Place**. There is general public access to the grounds (though bear in mind that it is a golf course), and the higher points afford panoramic views over Barnehurst to the north.

> May Place was originally built c1480, and was altered and extended over the centuries to become a large mansion. Its estate covered a vast area to the north and to the east. The grounds included the older Crayford Manor House, which eventually became just a farmhouse, its position usurped by May Place.
> By the 17th century May Place belonged to the Draper family, whose monument is the most outstanding in St Paulinus Church. In 1694 it was purchased by Admiral Sir Cloudesley Shovel, who died when his ship struck a rock off the Scilly Isles in 1707. Lady Shovel died in 1732, and her monument is also prominent in St Paulinus.
> In 1745 Miles Barne, a cloth merchant, arrived at May Place, and his family gave their name to two places in Crayford - Barnes Cray by 1800, and Barnehurst in 1895.

In 1903 a golf course was set up in the grounds, and May Place became the clubhouse. In 1938 Crayford UDC acquired the golf course and the Manor House *(see 37)*, which became a community centre in 1949. May Place was demolished after a fire in 1959, and the present clubhouse was built on the site.

Old walls from outbuildings, barns etc can still be seen to the east of the clubhouse. A footpath to the east leads to a lime tree avenue, probably dating back to the late 17th century, which was part of an early approach road to May Place and linked it to Crayford Manor House. A footpath continues to Perry Street along the line of the approach road, and another bears right round the grounds of the Manor House to emerge by the Stable Block in Mayplace Road East.

At the north-west corner of the course is a bank of trees, originally part of Old Manor Way, the old lane from Bexley to Erith. Old Manor Way is now a short road which passes under the railway bridge, still largely the original brick bridge of 1895.

37. *Crayford Manor House.* This highly attractive building was part of the May Place Estate; it is now a community centre, and is linked to the vast open space now occupied by the Barnehurst Golf Course *(see above)*.

> The earliest record of the Manor House goes back to the 14th century. May Place was built c1480 and became the home of the Lord of the Manor; it usurped the position of the Manor House, which became the farmhouse of a small farm attached to the May Place Estate. It was however still known as the Manor House.
>
> The house was rebuilt c1768 and again c1816 for members of the Barne family, but they ceased to live there after 1847. The house is featured in 'A Prisoner in Fairyland' by Algernon Blackwood, who was brought up there in the 1870s. It was acquired by Crayford UDC in 1938, and in 1949 it became a community centre.

The main part of this irregular stuccoed Italianate building was built c1816; it has an elegant iron verandah and balcony. The lower part at the east end remains from the previous building of c1768; the front entrance to this earlier building is now concealed behind a trellis enclosure, and is in poor condition.

To the left of the house is the **Observatory**, constructed in 1960 from an old boiler house; the prominent dome was added in 1982.

To the right of the house, accessible through an archway from the entrance drive, is the **stable block**, early 19th century though its appearance has been altered by the modern doors. From the rear of the stables a footpath bears left and leads to the lime tree avenue to May Place *(see above)*.

38. Oakwood Drive. The avenue of trees along this road used to lead to Oakwood, a mansion of 1849, demolished 1945; Mayplace School is now on the site. At the end of the road is an entrance to Martens Grove *(see below)*.

39. Martens Grove. An extensive park, oblong in shape, occupying part of the grounds of Martens Grove, a mansion of 1850 which was located in the park near the western end of Martens Avenue. It was demolished in 1932, and the Martens Grove Estate was then built on the grounds to the south, forming a close backcloth to the park.

The park embodies a variety of landscapes. Entering from the west at Spring Vale, there is a long ravine with steep and densely wooded sides; it then widens out into a flat grassed area, until 1989 the site of an open air swimming-pool. Beyond a finger of woodland on a steep slope continues to the east, eventually becoming a short lane leading out to Old Road near the junction with London Road.

CRAYFORD

Gazetteer

Section 'C' BARNES CRAY, THE SAW MILLS, WHITEHILL
(See map on page 14)

40. 1 Crayford Road, formerly called Whitehill House. A harmonious and attractive detached house with a fine portico, painted white, probably early 19th century.

Just outside the house, on the corner with Maiden Lane, is a **coal duty boundary marker**, a cast iron post of 1861 *(see introduction, page 13)*.

Two other such markers of 1861 are nearby. One is on the opposite side of the roundabout, on a grass embankment outside 8 Princes Road. Another is on the east side of Maiden Lane, just south of the railway bridge.

41. Whitehill Estate. The estate, consisting of Whitehill Road and adjoining sections of Maiden Lane and Crayford Road, was designed by Gordon Allen and built 1915-16 by Vickers to house munitions workers. The houses were mainly in groups of six, with two bold central archways each covering two recessed entrances. Many such groups have survived relatively unaltered, particularly in Whitehill Road.

42. Barnes Cray Fields. An area of wild marshland between the River Cray and the River Stanham, with the railway line running to the south and to the east. A footpath, part of the Cray Riverway, runs alongside the Cray.

> This area just south of the Cray was used for textile bleaching by both Swaisland and Applegath in the first half of the 19th century. An india-rubber factory was set up here c1847, and this was later changed to rug and carpet manufacturing which continued until 1885. No trace of this industrial activity now remains, nor of the mill on the river which was once here.

During the first world war the fields were used for Vickers workshops, with a railway siding from the Dartford Loop Line which also connected them to the main Vickers works. Some traces of the siding do remain - the railway embankment; the retaining brick walls of a former bridge over Maiden Lane (just north of the main railway bridge); and in the middle of the fields, the remains of a girder bridge.

The West Kent Main Sewer crosses the site, on both sides of the railway line, and penstock chambers and some old machinery can be seen on either side of the Cray.

43. *Barnes Cray Cottages, Maiden Lane. A fine terrace of farmworkers cottages c1695, though much altered and converted from five to three cottages; they were attached to Westbrook Farm, just north of the River Cray.

A driveway leads directly to other buildings c1695 remaining from the farm, which form an interesting ensemble around a square - the **farmhouse**, altered and extended, with a later porch facing east; a **barn** further east, largely in its original condition; to the right a building converted from another barn and reconstructed; and to the left a former slaughter-house.

44. *Barnes Cray Garden Village. This 'garden suburb' with over 600 houses, mostly concrete, was designed by Gordon Allen and built by Vickers 1915-16 to house munitions workers. It extends in a long rectangle between Iron Mill Lane and Crayford Way, stretching from Crayford town centre to Thames Road. Many houses have survived without major alterations, and despite later infill the estate retains a village atmosphere which is lacking in the other Vickers estates *(see 41, Erith 39)*.

The houses are in pairs and terraces, and common themes include prominent gables, recessed open porches, and roofs sweeping down so as to make the upper floor windows into dormers. Good groups can in particular be seen in Barnes Cray Road, Beech Walk, Village Green Road with the open space called **The Dell**, and the closes near the junction of Maiden Lane and Crayford Way.

A lane south from Beech Walk leads to the **Geoffrey Whitworth Theatre (44A)**, built 1959, red brick, with a fine, intimate interior. (Geoffrey Whitworth founded the British Drama League, and was a strong advocate of the 'little theatre'.)

45. 214/226 & 238/256 Iron Mill Lane. Two terraces of cottages with round-headed doorways, probably c1860, built to house workers at The Saw Mills industrial site.

46. The Jolly Farmers, Thames Road. An attractive pub, originally of 1830 but rebuilt in 1851, in classical style with massive stone quoins.

47. Crayford Flour Mill, Thames Road. The large white building, which is a local landmark, is of the 1950s. The factory still produces flour; although it bears the name Vitbe, it has not in fact produced Vitbe flour since 1962.

> This is the only reminder of the industrial area once called The Saw Mills *(see introduction, pages 10-11)*, where an iron mill had been set up in the 16th century. A corn mill was set up by the 17th century, on a site adjacent to the iron mill. In the 1760s the iron mill was replaced by a saw mill. Both corn mill and saw mill had their own water-wheel, and there was a large millpond. The corn mill was water-powered until 1909. It produced Vitbe flour from 1928 to 1962.

An old millstone has been set into the modern brick wall fronting Thames Road. The old millpond fed by the River Cray, though now much smaller, can be seen to the east of the factory, and quite a dramatic sluice falling about ten feet controls its flow; after this point the river becomes tidal and is called Crayford Creek.

48. Craymill Estate. A housing development of 1983 in an attractive vernacular style, with nice closes and pedestrian walks. Particularly attractive is the area in the centre around Craymill Square, where terraces with swooping slate roofs punctuated by rows of dormers face other terraces with slate facing between each storey.

49. Victoria Scott Court, Perry Street. The focal point of this housing development c1980 is a substantial and attractive Victorian Gothic building of 1868 (extended to the left, probably in the 1890s). It was formerly the Russell Stoneham Hospital, and was originally known as Orchard House.

It was at **Stonehams Pit**, just to the north at the end of Burgate Close off Wyatt Street, that a workshop of Old Stone Age flint implements was discovered in the 1880s under the brickearth *(see introduction, page 9)*.

CRAYFORD

Gazetteer

Section 'D' CRAYFORD MARSHES
(See map on page 28)

50. Railway viaducts. The brick viaducts crossing Thames Road and running behind the Crayford Flour Mill site are part of the North Kent Line, and were built by the South Eastern Railway to replace timber structures in 1863.

51. Coal duty boundary marker, a tall granite obelisk of 1851 *(see introduction, page 13)*. This unusual marker is in a field to the east of the railway line, by the River Stanham. It is best accessed by a lane alongside 229 Burnham Road.

52. *Cray, Darent & Thames - the Three Rivers Walk. The walk is well surfaced and runs for nearly five kilometres alongside the Rivers Cray (Crayford Creek), Darent (Dartford Creek) and Thames.

The footpath is on an embankment, which was raised and widened to its present level as part of the Thames flood defences carried out in the 1970s. It is in fact an enlargement of the **river wall** which was probably first constructed in the 14th century, and improved several times subsequently; some idea of the scale of the original project can be imagined.

The walk starts down a lane between Crayford Flour Mill and The Jolly Farmers, which then proceeds under the railway bridge and bears round sharply to the right to join the River Cray. Soon a sluice on the right controls the flow of the River Stanham into the Cray. The river is flanked by reed-beds, and at low tide is reduced to a narrow stream with mudflats exposed. To the left is the Crayford landfill site, looking quite barren and featureless, and bringing the land up to the level of the river wall. After nearly a kilometre the Cray joins the Darent, and after another similar distance the river sweeps to the left and is joined by a footpath from Howbury.

From here the landward views are more rewarding, and the river wall is embanked on both sides, for you have reached the ***Crayford Marshes** proper, with hedgerows, drainage ditches and grazing pastures. It is the most important area of marshland surviving on the south bank of the Thames to the west of Dartford Creek.

After nearly a kilometre there is a large warning notice: 'When this red light is flashing the Creek Flood Barrier is closed and vessels will be unable to pass through', and soon you reach the Dartford Creek Barrier *(see 53)*, where you have to cross stiles on either side of the approach road to the Barrier.

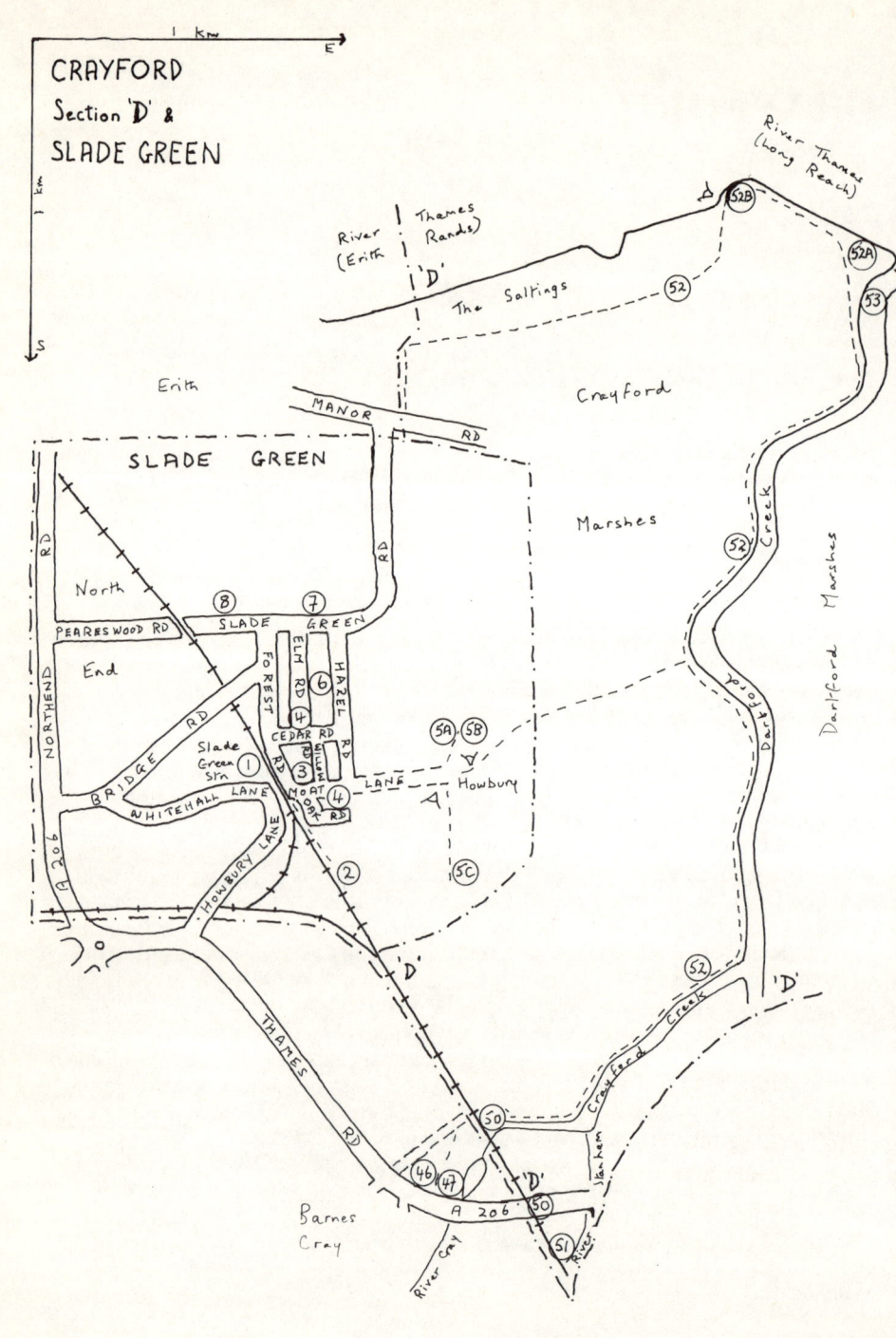

Continuing beyond the Barrier, the views are magnificent; to the right are views over Dartford Creek and the Dartford Marshes towards the Littlebrook Power Station of 1983, with the Queen Elizabeth II Bridge of 1991 (the longest cable-stayed bridge in Europe) in the distance.

When you reach the point at Long Reach where the Darent joins the Thames, it becomes very atmospheric, provided you ignore the ugly jumble of the industrial estate to your rear. Near this point, between the footpath and the river, though difficult to see from the footpath because of the falling levels of the land, is a **coal duty boundary marker (52A)**, a small stubby granite pillar of 1851 *(see introduction, page 13).*

Soon you come to the headland of ***Crayford Ness (52B)**, where there is a beacon and radar station, and a marvellous view westwards over Anchor Bay to Erith, with the tower block of Bexley College, the BICC tower and Erith Oil Works clearly visible.

The river wall now curves inland, with the saltmarshes known as The Saltings to the right. To the left, on the Marshes, are two small square brick tumps (or ammunition storage dumps) of the Thames Ammunition Works dating from the last war; further away are a pill-box and gun emplacements.

> The land around the Ness now occupied by the Thamesside Industrial Estate was from c1890 the site of the Thames Ammunition Works, which became part of Vickers Armstrong. During the first world war the works were extended to cover a large area of the Marshes, and were linked to the North Kent Line by a siding called the Trench Warfare Light Railway. The works finally closed c1962.

Eventually one reaches the Erith Yacht Club *(see Erith 11),* and the lane which leads up to Manor Road *(see Erith 10),* where the walk ends.

The walk can be shortened to about four kilometres by taking the Howbury footpath at the end of Moat Lane, Slade Green, turning left along the river wall, and finishing at Manor Road, Erith. The Howbury footpath can however get quite muddy and there are two stiles to negotiate, one of which may be found awkward.

It can be shortened further to about three kilometres by starting at Manor Road, Erith (take the lane beyond the industrial premises on the north side of the road), walking to the Dartford Creek Barrier, and then retracing steps. This walk covers the main points of interest - Crayford Ness, the coal duty marker, and the Barrier - and has the advantage of returning to the starting-point.

53. *Dartford Creek Barrier. This flood barrier across the mouth of Dartford Creek, just before it joins the Thames, was built by Sir Bruce White, Wolfe Barry & Partners, and completed in 1982. It consists of two massive concrete piers linked by a bridge 30 metres wide; housed under the bridge are two falling radial gates, one above the other, which when dropped together can close the whole depth of the Creek, thus preventing a high surge tide from the Thames posing a flood threat to Crayford and Dartford.

The barrier can be reached at the end of Maypole Crescent on the Thamesside Industrial Estate, but the scrapyard activity all around makes this access, whether by car or on foot, rather unpleasant. So, even though this involves a much longer walk, it is worth considering access from the Howbury footpath or from Manor Road, Erith (see above).

CRAYFORD

Suggested Walks

It is recommended that the suggested walks be followed in conjunction with the Gazetteer and the map (on page 14), and that the Gazetteer be consulted at each location for a detailed description. Most locations described in Sections 'A' and 'C' of the Gazetteer, and all locations in Section 'B', are included; some locations are not included, as they might add too much to the length of the walks. The walks follow a more or less circular route, so can be joined at any location. Section 'D' is not covered, as the walk along the river wall of the Cray, Darent & Thames is described in the gazetteer. Walks Nos 1 & 3 begin and end at Crayford Station, and Walk No 2 at Barnehurst Station.

WALK No 1 (including the old Vickers works, Crayford Bridge, the High Street, St Paulinus Church, Orchard Hill). Distance approx two kilometres.

NB. For information on viewing the interiors of St Paulinus Church and St Mary of the Crays Church, see the gazetteer.

SECTION 'A'. On leaving **Crayford Station (1)**, proceed east to **Station Road (3)** and turn right. Note **The Royal Charlotte (3A)**, **nos 78/82** and **no 88 (3B)**, then retrace steps; cross the bridge over the railway, and note the Thames Water installation **(3E)** on the right. On reaching Crayford Road, turn left and note **Crayford Town Hall (4)**.

Cross the road to the **Clock Tower (6)**; go into the **Rich Industrial Estate (7)** to see the old Vickers buildings, following the route described in the Gazetteer, then return to the Clock Tower and turn right. Continue to **Crayford Bridge (8)**; note **The Bear & Ragged Staff (9)** ahead. Proceed straight ahead up **Crayford High Street**, keeping to the right-hand side of the road. Note **nos 25/35 (10)** and **The Crayford Arms (11)** on the opposite side, then **Grove Place (12)** on this side. Opposite, at the top, are **The One Bell** and **172/6 Old Road (13)**.

Turn right, and immediately right again, into **Iron Mill Lane**, noting **no 8a, the Priests House, Mrs Stables Almshouses** and **nos 18/20 (14)**. Cross the road to **St Paulinus School (15)**, and bear left to **Mr Pims Almshouses (16)**. Continue, turn right, and cross the road to the **Church of St Paulinus (17)**; try to see the interior.

Leave the churchyard by the lych-gate and proceed straight ahead down Manor Road to **St Mary of the Crays Church (18)**; try to see the interior, and note the old building of St Josephs School. Go down **Chapel Hill** to the left of the church, turn right into **Star Hill**, then left down **Orchard Hill (21)**. Turn left to **Crayford Baptist Church (22)**, and continue along **Bexley Lane**, noting **nos 56/64 (23)** and **no 38 (24)**. Cross the road, and return along Bexley Lane to **The Duke of Wellington (25)**.

Facing you is the **Bourne Industrial Park (26)**, with the **Long Shed (26A)**, and to the right the old wall of Bexley House, and Crest House. If you have time, go through the entrance, and visit the exhibition at the **David Evans works (26B)**.

From the Long Shed, proceed east along London Road, noting **Wolsley Close (27)** and **nos 4/6 (28)**, to Crayford Bridge, then continue along Crayford Road, turn right into Station Road and back to Crayford Station.

WALK No 2 (including Barnehurst, the Golf Course, Crayford Manor House, and Martens Grove). Distance approx four kilometres.

It is worth trying to make an advance arrangement - see the gazetteer - to view the interior of St Martins Church. Bear in mind that parts of the footpath by the Golf Course can get muddy.

SECTION 'B'. On leaving **Barnehurst Station (31)**, turn right along Barnehurst Road, passing **The Red Barn (32)**, to the road junction. **Bursted Wood (33)** is opposite. Turn left down Erith Road until you reach **St Martins Church (34)**; try to see the interior.

Continue along Erith Road, and turn left along Mayplace Road East. Note **Sarahs Cottages (35)** opposite. After Manor Way, you reach the entrance to **Barnehurst Golf Course (36)**; turn left along the entrance drive to the **Clubhouse (36A)**. Continue along the footpath to the lime tree avenue, and then take the footpath which bears right to emerge by the Stable Block of **Crayford Manor House (37)**.

From the Manor House, turn right along Mayplace Road East until you reach **Oakwood Drive (38)** opposite; go down this road and into **Martens Grove (39)**. If you have time, go downhill into the Park. Otherwise, keep to the right along the footpaths, and you will emerge back on Mayplace Road East. Barnehurst Road is opposite, leading back to Barnehurst Station.

WALK No 3 (including Whitehill, Barnes Cray and The Saw Mills). Distance approx four kilometres.

On leaving **Crayford Station (1)**, proceed east to Station Road and turn left. On reaching Crayford Road, turn right.

SECTION 'C'. Just before reaching Princes Road, note the **coal duty boundary marker** on the grass embankment above the pavement. Cross the road by the roundabout, and note **1 Crayford Road (40)** and the **coal duty marker** outside by the junction with Maiden Lane. Proceed along Maiden Lane; look down Whitehill Road, where houses of the **Whitehill Estate (41)** have been least altered. Note the **coal duty marker** on the right before going under the railway bridge.

Note the brick walls of the former bridge of the Vickers railway siding, and then **Barnes Cray Fields (42)** to the right. Cross the River Cray, and note **Barnes Cray Cottages (43)** and the farm buildings behind. You have now reached **Barnes Cray Garden Village (44)**.

Cross the road and follow Barnes Cray Road as it bears right and crosses Crayford Way. Note **The Dell**, and the houses round it, then turn right into Beech Walk. Take the lane on the right to the **Geoffrey Whitworth Theatre (44A)**. Continue along Beech Walk, turn left into Maiden Lane, and right along **Iron Mill Lane**.

At the end note the two terraces, **nos 214/226 & 238/256 (45)**, and **The Jolly Farmers (46)** and **Crayford Flour Mill (47)** opposite. (Cross the road to see the millpond.) Bear right along Crayford Way. Note the two closes just before crossing Maiden Lane. Continue the whole length of Crayford Way until you reach Crayford Bridge, turn left into Crayford Road, and right into Station Road back to the Station.

SLADE GREEN

Gazetteer

(See map on page 28)

1. Slade Green Station. This station on the North Kent Line was not opened until 1900, though the line first ran through in 1849. The present building is of 1968. A mural showing the railway history of Slade Green has been removed for restoration.

From the footbridge over the line there is a good view to the south of the diverging railway lines - the main North Kent Line to Dartford of 1849 is straight ahead, the line to the left of 1901 leads into the maintenance depot, and the line to the right of 1895 links up with the Bexleyheath Line.

2. Slade Green Railway Maintenance Depot, an extensive workshop and train shed complex, accessed by a private road opposite the Station. First one comes to the original engine inspection shed, opened 1901, with its series of round-headed arches. The shed beyond was opened as a repair shop in 1925, and was extended in 1937; it has recently been modernised to become the main depot for Networker trains for this part of Network South-East.

> The site is not open to the public, and the engine sheds are not visible from the entrance. However, there is a good though distant view from Moat Lane, at the beginning of the private road to Howbury Grange (see 5).

3. The Railway Tavern, a handsome pub of 1900. Note the line of Doric columns rounding the frontage, and the open balcony on the corner.

4. Railway Estate, an extensive estate built 1900 by the South East & Chatham Railway for workers at Slade Green Railway Depot. The houses in Oak Road and Moat Lane are mostly in groups of four, with canopied doorways and flanking walls projecting above the roof as a parapet; whereas the houses in Hazel Road (west side), Cedar Road and Elm Road are mostly in groups of six, with central projecting bays. A terrace in Willow Road was added in 1904.

5. **Howbury. This area has a special atmosphere, and is remarkable for the survival of the 12th century moat walls of the Manor House, and of a 17th century barn.

> Howbury was a manor by the reign of Edward the Confessor; it later became part of the May Place estate. It was held by the Draper family in the 17th century. Admiral Sir Cloudesley Shovel bought it in 1694, and it was held by his family until 1778. The manor house was inhabited until 1935, and has since become a ruin. A brick bridge was built to replace a drawbridge over the moat c1780; it collapsed in 1963.

At the eastern end of Moat Lane, three ways diverge - to the left is a short private road to Howbury Barn; ahead over a stile is the Howbury footpath, a public footpath to Dartford Creek; and to the right is a private road to Howbury Grange. At this point, to the right is a good but distant view across the fields to Howbury Grange and the

Clock Tower (1902) - *Crayford 6*

Crayford Town Hall (1915) - *Crayford 4*

The One Bell (early 19th century) - *Crayford 13*

Church of St Paulinus (12th / 15th century) - *Crayford 17*

38 Bexley Lane (early 19th century) - *Crayford 24*

Crayford Manor House (c1768, c1816) - *Crayford 37*

Barnes Cray Cottages (c1695) - *Crayford 43*

1 Crayford Road (early 19th century) & coal duty marker (1861) - *Crayford 40*

Beech Walk, Barnes Cray Garden Village (Gordon Allen, 1915-16) - *Crayford 44*

The Jolly Farmers (1851) & Crayford Flour Mill (1950s)- *Crayford 46 / 47*

Dartford Creek Barrier (Sir Bruce White, Wolfe Barry, 1982) - *Crayford 53*

Moat walls, Howbury Manor House (12th century) - *Slade Green 5B*

Erith Station (1849) - *Erith 1*

Stone Court (1985 replicas of late 18th century cottages) - *Erith 6*

St John the Baptist Church (12th / 14th century, 1877
Erith 18

The Nordenfeldt (1902) -
Erith 21

**Our Lady of the Angels Church
(1963)** - *Erith 28*

**Belvedere Methodist Church
(1876)** - *Belvedere 5*

Milton Road (probably 1870s) - *Belvedere 7*

The Old Leather Bottle (late 18th century) - *Belvedere 8*

All Saints Church (William & Edward Habershon 1853) - *Belvedere 19*

All Saints Vicarage (1853) - *Belvedere 20*

Silos at Erith Oil Works (Christiani & Nielsen 1916) - *Belvedere 30*

BICC cable cooling tower (1992) -
Belvedere 31

Lesnes Abbey, the abbey church (1178-1200) - *Abbey Wood 1*

Lesnes Abbey, the cloisters (1178-1200) - *Abbey Wood 1*

Abbey Wood Station (1975) - *Abbey Wood 3*

Shopping Centre (1986)
Clock Tower (1762, 1987)
Thamesmead 1

Thamesmere Pumping Station (c1976) - *Thamesmead 2B*

Crossway Lake & Tump 39 - *Thamesmead 19*

Wren Path (1984) - *Thamesmead 31*

Broadwater Lock (1814) - *Thamesmead 32A*

original railway shed of 1901; to the left one can see Howbury Cottages, and there is a not very satisfactory view of Howbury Barn.

Taking the private road to the left, first one comes to **Howbury Cottages**, a terrace of three cottages of 1880, on the right. Then on the left is *****Howbury Tithe Barn (5A)**, a fine large early 17th century barn of red brick, with two projecting wagon entrances; the slits served as ventilation and to prevent birds flying in. The two separate ranges to the south are later; at the end of the left-hand range creepers cover the ruin of an oast-house.

Opposite on the right are the stone ****moat walls of Howbury Manor House (5B)**, basically 12th century, well preserved and still surrounded by a moat. The scanty remaining ruins (mainly a section of the south wall) of the last Howbury Manor House, built in the 17th century, can be seen under the creepers.

The public footpath ahead gives a rather better view of the moat walls and moat, and from here they look extremely picturesque. The view is best in the winter, but in the summer there are still views through gaps in the hedge. One can also see Howbury Barn, but the view is unsatisfactory because of the modern ranges in front.

The Howbury footpath continues to Dartford Creek, joining the Three Rivers Walk *(see Crayford 52)*. It can get quite muddy and there are two stiles to negotiate, one of which may be found awkward.

The private road to the right leads to **Howbury Grange (5C)**, which is on the site of a Saxon settlement. The Grange is now the office of the Russell Stoneham Estate (which owns much of Howbury and the Crayford Marshes). It is a large and imposing house of 1880, multi-gabled with Gothic entrance and window arches. The former stables and coach-house are also of 1880. The road gives excellent views across the fields to the Slade Green Railway Maintenance Depot.

For those with a serious interest in viewing more closely the moat walls, Howbury Barn & Howbury Grange, it may be worth contacting Mr Colin Stoneham, Russell Stoneham Estate, Howbury Grange, Moat Lane, DA8 2NE, 01322 333111, to ask for permission.

6. The Lord Raglan, Hazel Road. A pleasant classical building, originally mid 19th century, rebuilt c1900.

7. Slade Green School. The building fronting the road, with Gothic doorways and windows, was the Slade Green National School of 1868. The section to the left was the teacher's house.

8. Church of St Augustine, Slade Green Road. A bulky, rather ungainly Gothic church of 1900 redeemed by a nice belfry. The aisles and a new porch were added in 1911, when the west end was extended by two bays. The church has been much rebuilt because of war and fire damage.

The interior *(contact The Vicarage, Slade Green Road, 01322 333970)* is more imposing, with fine Gothic arcades. Note the vivid red brick arches along the arcades and over the windows. The colourful stained glass in the apse windows and at the west end of the south aisle is postwar.

The handsome **Vicarage** next door looks mid 19th century, but is actually of 1923.

ERITH

Introduction

Erith is a riverside industrial town, situated in a bay sheltered within a bend of the Thames. It is flanked to the east by the Crayford Marshes, still mostly surviving, and to the west by the Erith Marshes, now largely covered by the Belvedere Industrial Area and Thamesmead. Before the construction (probably in the 14th century) of a river embankment to protect the marshes, Erith was one of few places on the south side of the Thames between Greenwich and the Estuary which could be used as a landing-place.

It has never really become a typical outer London suburb; the residential streets near the centre (despite much modern housing) seem to remain Victorian and Edwardian in atmosphere. The suburbs start to the south at Northumberland Heath.

Erith deserves a better town centre. Its concrete shopping centre has a brutal impact, and the once busy area around the High Street is now desolate and cut off from the river by the totally unused Erith Deep Wharf. To the west, however, is a short but fine sequence of buildings which are virtually all that remains of the old High Street. Beyond, the Riverside Gardens and Promenade are a disappointment, with the river not visible from the gardens and the gardens not visible from the walk.

This introduction is extended to cover the area of Belvedere, which was once part of Erith parish and borough.

Early history

Although prehistoric and Roman finds have been made in the Erith area, the earliest indication of any settled community dates from the Saxon period. St John the Baptist Church, the original parish church, is on the site of a Saxon church.

Its location is not in the present town centre, but a kilometre away to the west where the Bedon stream, now underground, joins the Thames; at this point the ridge of hills which stretches for five kilometres from Bostall Woods comes down to river level.

The earliest parts of the present church are Norman, c1100. Later in the 12th century Lesnes Abbey, part of the same manor as Erith, was founded three kilometres away to the west. There was a medieval manor house, probably c1180, near the church; its foundations were excavated in 1994, but are on the route of the Thamesmead to Erith Spine Road, construction of which will start shortly.

The Tudor period

The first major event to shift the focus of Erith to its present location was the foundation by Henry VIII of a naval dockyard at the eastern end of West Street. The Great Harry, built at Woolwich in 1514, was fitted out at Erith the same year. But, unlike those at Deptford and Woolwich, the dockyard at Erith remained in use for only a few years, as the surrounding land was not found suitable for expansion.

Henry VIII granted the manor of Erith to the Countess of Shrewsbury, and her monument is the finest in St Johns Church. His reign also saw the end of the Abbey at Lesnes, dissolved by Cardinal Wolsey in 1525 before the Reformation.

Early Victorian Erith

In the early 19th century Erith was still a small riverside town; though separated by fields from its parish church, it had continued to develop near the site of the Tudor dockyard. There was a wharf on the site of Riverside Gardens, which was used also by the Admiralty.

Just to the west Lower Ballast Wharf (later called Railway Station Wharf) had been used from c1805 for loading ballast and loam from Parish's Pits. In 1842 a new Ballast Wharf was constructed upstream, with its own railway to Parish's Pits.

Also in 1842 a scheme to turn the area now occupied by Erith Deep Wharf into a resort for river steamers was initiated, and a hotel, gardens and a long pier were constructed. The scheme was not a success, and after industrial development had started in the 1860s, it was finally abandoned in 1874.

The North Kent Line reached Erith in 1849, and the residential development of the Lesney Park Estate began in 1854. More importantly, in the 1860s industrial activity began to expand to the east of the town, linked by a siding to the railway beyond Erith Station. From this time Erith was destined to become an industrial centre.

The industrial town

The dock and wharves of Anchor Bay in East Erith were used in the 1860s for the export of bricks manufactured from the brickearth deposits going south towards Slade Green, and of the products of the Erith Ironworks of Easton & Anderson, the first major manufacturing industry in Erith, which opened in 1864.

The great names of industrial Erith - BICC, Vickers, Fraser & Chalmers - had all been established by 1893. Despite the many industries which have gone, Erith is still a busy industrial centre.

Industrial Erith can now be divided into three zones - Fraser Road, and the riverside on either side of the town centre. The riverside to the west, mostly in Belvedere, is now the most important, but each zone has played an important part in Erith's industrial history.

The eastern riverside

Manor Road stretches east from the town centre, cut off from the river by a varied and not always pleasant series of industrial sites. The dock of Anchor Bay is still there, now on the Costains site. From the 1860s until the first world war, it was linked by a network of railway sidings to brickworks, manufacturing mostly London stock bricks, and also to the Erith Ironworks of Easton & Anderson.

Easton & Anderson opened at Anchor Bay in 1864, and the works occupied extensive premises along the river. Many steam engines were manufactured, but it closed in 1904. From 1911 Anchor Bay was used for importing coal and other commodities by Herbert Clarke, a firm of barge owners established in the 1890s.

Nearer the town centre is Erith Deep Wharf, a vast derelict area. This was the site of the failed riverside resort, which had begun in 1842. In 1874 it turned to industrial use. Associated Newspapers now own it, but it has lain abandoned since 1989.

The western riverside

The western riverside zone stretches from Erith town centre for nearly five kilometres, embracing the Belvedere riverside area; it ends at the Crossness Sewage Works, now a modern works of 1964, but including the old works of 1865 which are in the early stages of restoration. The two most important factories still in operation in this zone are BICC (British Insulated Callenders Cables) and Erith Oil Works, both accessible from Church Manorway.

The forerunners of BICC moved to their first major works here in 1880. Manufacture of cables was at first a sideline to bitumen products, but it soon became the factory's main activity. By 1965 the site here was the principal manufacturing unit of the world's largest cable group.

The Erith Oil Works, founded 1908, are remarkable for the bank of 24 silos of 1916, the first major example of reinforced concrete in this country.

Other well-known names in this zone which have closed include Doulton, which made stoneware pipes from c1927 to 1974; and Borax, established 1899 but demolished 1994, now the proposed site for the Cory waste-to-energy incinerator.

Fraser Road

Fraser Road was laid out c1895. The area to its north, now the Europa Industrial Estate, had been from c1805 quarried for stone ballast, sand and loam by Parish's Pits (as it became known). By the time two of the most important firms in Erith's history arrived on the site, Nordenfeldt (later to become Vickers) in 1887 and Fraser & Chalmers in 1893, it had been exhaustively quarried. However, quarrying continued in the area now known as Erith Quarry on the other side of Fraser Road until c1971.

In 1887 the Nordenfeldt Gun & Ammunition Co acquired part of the site. In 1888 it merged with the Maxim Company, and in 1897 it was purchased by Vickers and became VSM (Vickers Son & Maxim). During the Boer Wars the works employed 4000 persons producing machine guns In 1911 the Erith works commenced the manufacture of aircraft, and most early Vickers aircraft were constructed at Erith. After the war the Erith works diversified into various peacetime products, but it closed in 1931 and production was transferred to Crayford.

In 1893 the American engineering firm of Fraser & Chalmers commenced production of mining and milling machinery here, and from 1907 it became a major manufacturer of steam engines. In 1937 the adjoining Vickers factory was purchased, and it controlled virtually the whole site. GEC, which had acquired Fraser & Chalmers in 1918, continued to use part of the site until the 1980s.

Residential development

The building of large houses in Erith did not take off until after the opening of Erith Station in 1849. The Wheatley family, whose manor house was at the head of Avenue Road, began to develop the Lesney Park Estate in the grounds.

The first houses were built along the south side of Bexley Road in the 1850s, and along the north side in the 1860s. Although the roads of the Estate were laid out by 1860, only a few houses were built initially. The main housing development did not start till after the Wheatley Estate was sold in 1874, and even then much of thè area had not been developed by 1900. A new church, Christ Church, was built for the estate in 1874; later its interior was largely covered with remarkable paintings and murals, and a landmark steeple added.

The heathland of Northumberland Heath had been enclosed in 1815, but its development for housing did not begin until the 1860s and did not really accelerate until the 1880s. An estate for Vickers workers was built there in 1916. The rest of the area was developed in the 1920s and 1930s.

Lower and Upper Belvedere

In the early 19th century there was already a hamlet called Picardy at Lower Belvedere, near the junction of Picardy Street and Picardy Road. About a kilometre to the south there were a number of buildings at the southern end of Nuxley Road, leading down to the hamlet of Bedonwell, by the source of the Bedon stream. In between lay the mansion of Belvedere House (first built c1740), with substantial grounds leading downhill towards Erith, and an area of heathland called Lessness Heath. This heathland was to become part of the Belvedere Estate, now called Upper Belvedere.

Lord Eardley of Belvedere House had secured the enclosure of Lessness Heath in 1815. Sir Culling Eardley, who inherited Belvedere House in 1847, built a parish church and vicarage in 1853; he laid out the Heath and other parts of his estate to the north in building plots in 1856, and once Belvedere Station opened in 1859, the development of the Belvedere Estate began very quickly. In the 1860s a number of large houses were constructed in the area, and the development also began to stretch down towards Picardy.

Belvedere House was sold in 1865 and became a home for elderly seamen. In 1959 the old mansion was replaced by a large modern block, but this was in turn replaced by housing in the early 1980s; the eastern part of the grounds remained largely open space as Frank's Park, first acquired by Erith Council in 1920.

The hamlet of Picardy disappeared with the development of Lower Belvedere, which began with smaller houses in the 1880s. Two pubs, the Leather Bottle (which may date back to the 17th century) and the Prince Alfred, are now on side roads, but were originally on the main road, which ran via St Augustines Road, Abbey Crescent and Picardy Road; Gilbert Road and Picardy Street were not built until the 1880s.

Belvedere is an area of great character, with an irregular and intriguing network of roads, where many varied and distinctive Victorian houses have survived. Its location astride the ridge formed by Woolwich Road and Erith Road ensures fine views from many points.

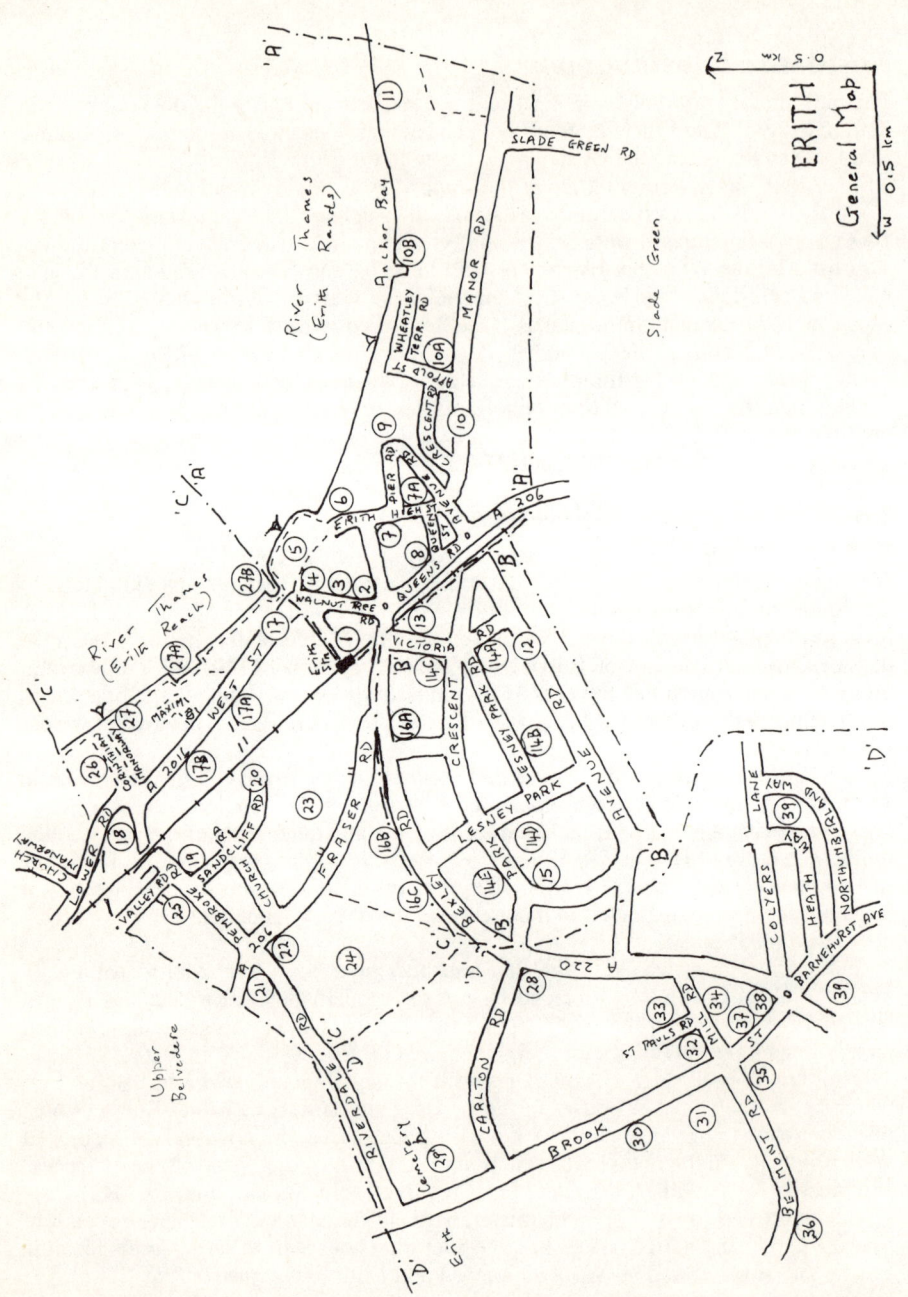

ERITH

Gazetteer

Section 'A' CENTRAL & EAST ERITH

1. ***Erith Station**, Stonewood Road. The original brick station building of the North Kent Line of 1849 has survived, and has recently been restored. It is elegant and harmonious, with a central round-headed doorway. Note the unusual staggered platforms.

2. **Erith Town Hall**, a classical building of 1931, with portico and pilasters; the top floor was added c1990. It was the town hall of Erith Urban District Council until 1938, and of Erith Borough Council until 1965, when the London Borough of Bexley was created. It is now used as council offices; ask permission to see the old council chamber upstairs, a wide semi-circular room with a dome in the ceiling.

3. **Erith Library**, Walnut Tree Road. An amazing quixotic building of 1906, with a classical portico echoed in the tiny niche above, oval windows along the upper floor, and a weird cupola with a weathervane in the shape of a ship on top. Note on the porch floor the old Erith Council coat-of-arms in mosaic with the motto 'Labour overcomes all things'.

On the first floor is **Erith Museum** *(open Mondays & Wednesdays 1415 to 1715, Saturdays 1415 to 1700)*. It is a small museum, with display-cases on the history of Erith, particularly archaeological and industrial; there is some Roman pottery, a reconstruction of an Edwardian kitchen, and models of the Great Harry and of Hiram Maxim's flying machine.

4. **Riverside Swimming Centre**. A modernist building by Richard Seifert of 1968; the north wall is glazed. A large coloured mural panel by William Mitchell on the side shows themes from Erith's history, including Richard de Lucy and the murder of Thomas a Becket, the stern of an East India Co ship, the Countess of Shrewsbury, and The Great Harry.

Adjacent in Walnut Tree Road is the former **Electricity Generating Station**. Originally built 1903, mainly for street lighting, and considerably enlarged in 1905 for Erith Council Tramways, it continued in use to 1927, when it was replaced by cables from Woolwich Power Station. The site is now in use as Erith Sub-Station.

> Erith Council Tramways started operations in 1905, with routes to Abbey Wood, Northumberland Heath, and North End. The depot and tram-shed were in the great pit on the opposite side of Walnut Tree Road. The tramways closed down in 1935, but the depot building was not demolished until 1980.

5. Riverside Gardens. A small but rather formal park laid out in 1937, enlarged 1982, but providing no proper view of the river.

Below the gardens is a riverside walkway, **William Cory Promenade**; it is disappointing as one is hardly aware of the gardens behind, and the view down-river is occluded by the green corrugated-iron covered jetty of Erith Deep Wharf *(see 9)*. However, there are good views across the river to Coldharbour Point, where a small red lighthouse can be seen, and the Rainham and Wennington Marshes. At the eastern end is a modern wooden jetty of the PLA, used as a landing-place for small boats. At the western end is the dock of Railway Station Wharf, and the riverside walk westwards *(see 27)*.

Across the road from the gardens is the rather striking mock-Jacobean **Running Horses**, a pub of 1937.

6. *Erith High Street. A short but fine sequence of buildings remains from the old High Street. From west to east:

Erith Police Station. The building on the riverside, used by the river police until 1994, is now the police station. The original police station on the High Street, an attractive and dignified building in red brick of 1908, is no longer in police use.

***Stone Court.** This housing development of 1985 incorporates replicas of a pair of white late 18th century cottages, which were on the site; they were very well reconstructed as part of the development. To the rear, a raised walkway above the gardens gives a good view of the rear of the cottages, and leads to a large modern red brick block of 1985.

The Cross Keys. A fantastic extravaganza of 1892, large and tall, with an elaborate arabesque plasterwork frieze, corner turret, recessed balconies, and all sorts of weird decoration.

Erith Playhouse, a pleasing theatre of 1973. It replaced a theatre of 1949, which started as the Oxford Cinema of 1913.

The White Hart, a handsome pub, going back at least to the early 18th century, its present frontage of 1902. The rear garden gives a distant view of the river, and has a small aviary and menagerie.

7. Town Centre. The shopping centre, called **Town Square**, is a pedestrianised precinct by Richard Seifert of 1968, concrete and very unappealing, in fact quite frightful and depressing, particularly where the access ramp to the roof-top car park crosses over Erith High Street.

Behind is **Erith Market**, an open air market, operating Wednesdays and Saturdays. There had been a market at Erith in medieval times, but it had fallen into disuse by the early 19th century. The market on the present site was opened c1980.

In the desolate triangle of streets **(7A)** between the shopping centre and Erith Deep Wharf, only three buildings now stand out above the wilderness:

Mecca Bingo Club, formerly the Odeon cinema, of 1938, retaining its cream faienced tiling, and with an unusual tower.

Erith Trades and Social Club, Avenue Road, a dignified red brick building of 1908, originally called the Erith Amalgamated Engineers and Allied Trades Club and Institute.

Bank Chambers, Pier Road, the head office of Herbert Clarke *(see 10)*, c1900.

8. Queen Street Baptist Church. Two buildings in similar Gothic style, with twin pinnacles above the entrances and lots of lancet windows. The smaller building, to the right, is the original church of 1877, now the church hall; the larger, to the left, is the present church of 1892.

9. Erith Deep Wharf. The site is large, extending from the bottom of Pier Road to the bottom of Appold Street. The present concrete pier and jetty are of 1957. It has been owned since 1967 by Associated Newspapers, but the site has not been in use since 1989. There is no public access, though there is a view from the Ready Mixed Concrete site at Wheatley Terrace Road *(ask for permission to go down to the riverfront).*

> This was the site of riverside gardens, a hotel and a long pier, all constructed in 1842. This attempted resort did not work, and the site became industrial in 1874 as an extension to the already existing Cray Coal Wharf of 1864; the wharf became known as Railway Pier when used by William Cory for coal imports and a coal depot from 1899.

From 1864 a railway siding used to run from the North Kent Line to Cray Coal Wharf, with later branches into the coal depot and the Erith Ironworks of Easton & Anderson. The disused track-bed of the siding can still be seen from the road bridge at the western end of Manor Road. Rail tracks of the coal depot branch can be seen over the wall in Crescent Road, and the disused track-bed of the Ironworks branch from the road bridge in Appold Street.

10. Manor Road runs parallel with, but provides no view of the river. The western end is residential; on the north side are long terraces of cottages of 1866, built largely for workers at Easton & Anderson, and a pub **The Royal Alfred (10A)**, also c1866. Behind these terraces is part of the derelict Erith Deep Wharf.

Beyond the houses, the road is largely lined by modern industrial premises; but its industrial past was based on the **Anchor Bay dock (10B)** and Anchor Bay Wharf alongside.

> South of Manor Road as far as Slade Green there were from c1860 to the first world war extensive brickworks, manufacturing largely London Stock bricks. North of Manor Road from 1864 to 1904 was the Erith Ironworks of Easton & Anderson, occupying extensive premises along the river; its main products were steam engines and, later, electrical machinery. Between 1911 and the last war the Ironworks site was used as a coal wharf by Herbert Clarke, a firm of barge owners established in the 1890s. The products of the brickworks and of the Ironworks were exported from Anchor Bay, which dates back at least to the mid 19th century.

Anchor Bay dock and Anchor Bay Wharf are still there, on the Costain site *(ask at reception for permission to view).* For remains of railway sidings in the area, *see 9.*

11. Erith Yacht Club, The Saltings. Accessible by a narrow lane (which can become muddy) beyond the industrial premises on the north side of Manor Road.

> The Royal Corinthian Yacht Club was at the end of Corinthian Manorway from 1872 to 1898. The premises were taken over by Erith Yacht Club in 1901, and they moved to this site in 1929.

From here a footpath leads along the embanked river wall, with saltmarshes to the left and Crayford Marshes to the right, to Crayford Ness and the Dartford Creek Barrier, and eventually to Crayford Flour Mill at Crayford Creek *(see Crayford 52).*

ERITH

Gazetteer

Section 'B' LESNEY PARK
(See map on page 38)

12. Avenue Road. This wide avenue, lined by grass verges and lime trees, is stately and impressive. It was first laid out c1769 as an approach road to the newly built Manor House of William Wheatley; the house was demolished 1858, its site now occupied by the postwar Erith School. Housing development started c1880, but of the early housing only an Edwardian group, nos 28/58, survive. Most buildings are now interwar and postwar, and do not measure up to the character of the road.

13. Christ Church, Victoria Road. A large Victorian Gothic brick church, with a virtually detached brick clock-tower and tall stone spire which is a landmark for the area. It is situated in a fine large churchyard, forming a pleasant green.

The main church was built in 1874 by James Piers St Aubyn, and the tower and spire (also to a design by St Aubyn) added in 1915.

The exterior is grand, but rather uninspired; the *interior (contact the Vicarage next door in Victoria Road, 01322 334729)* is something else. Note first the imposing chancel arch, the short round nave piers with elaborate capitals, the sharply pointed arches of the arcades, the high hammerbeam roof, and the attractive patterned brickwork. Note also the five richly coloured stained glass lancets by John Hardman at the east end. All these belong to the original church.

But in 1906-09 much of the interior was covered in paintings and other decoration by Ward & Hughes. The paintings along the aisles, which are on canvas, are particularly interesting, featuring scenes from early Kentish religious history. Elsewhere - in the chancel, on the wall at the west end, and above the chancel arch - the murals are painted directly on the bricks. Many of the paintings are somewhat faded now, but the effect is still quite extraordinary. Note also, as part of the reredos, the painted tryptich of the Adoration of the Magi, 1904.

To the rear is the old **Sunday School**, built c1892, large red brick with Gothic arches and wheel windows.

14. *Lesney Park Estate. The estate was laid out soon after William Wheatley's Manor House was demolished in 1858. Some houses in the new roads were built in the early 1860s, but the housing development did not really start until after the Wheatley Estate was sold in 1874, and even then much of the area had not been developed by 1900. The road network comprises Bexley Road (where houses had been built from 1854 - *see 16)*, Park Crescent and Lesney Park Road, with the linking roads of Lesney Park, Victoria Road and Park Crescent Road; Avenue Road had been laid out c1769 *(see 12)*, and Christchurch Avenue is postwar infill. The road layout, with its grass verges, drainage channels and trees, is quite splendid, and some of the Victorian houses have individual and intriguing decorative details. Note in particular:

1/3 Lesney Park Road (14A), of 1861, long and low with projecting parapetted bays.

5 & 7 Lesney Park Road, probably late 1870s, similar detached houses, with intricate patterns carved into the stonework.

Hainault (14B), 35/37 Lesney Park Road, probably of the 1880s, a large and unusual house with a strange porch and prominent gables.

76/78 Park Crescent (14C), of 1863, large and imposing, of bright red brick.

173 Park Crescent (14D), of 1861, formerly called Riversfield, accessible by a short lane, with an imposing ornamental carved porch topped by a tower. **83 Lesney Park**, probably of the late 1870s, with much ornamental detail, was a lodge for the house.

226 Park Crescent (14E), of 1861, with parapets and deep eaves.

15. Erith Hospital, Park Crescent. An exotic Cape Dutch style building of 1924, with an elaborate Dutch shaped gable in the centre. It is linked to a larger neo-Georgian block of 1935 on the right, which also has a shaped gable over the entrance echoing the much larger one in the main building.

16. Bexley Road climbs gradually as it curves round on its way from the Erith Town Centre to Northumberland Heath. A series of large houses were built along the south side in the 1850s; only **nos 63/65 (16A)**, a solid building of 1854, survives. The north side was developed in the 1860s, and of this **no 88 (16B)**, a handsome house of 1861, with deep eaves and intriguing round-headed windows, and **St Marys (16C)**, no 106, of 1862, survive.

ERITH

Gazetteer

Section 'C' WEST ERITH
(See map on page 38)

17. West Street leads from the town centre to the old parish church, between the railway line and the riverside. It begins with terraces of late 19th century houses, and ends with large vernacular-style housing developments of the 1990s. Work on the Thamesmead to Erith Spine Road is shortly to commence to the north of the railway line, and is due for completion in 1997.

The riverside walk *(see 27)* is accessible at either end of West Street, but also midway along, from a small green space with a footpath leading to Ballast Wharf.

On the left **Nordenfeldt Road (17A)** is a lane leading under the railway bridge to connect with Sandcliff Road *(see 20)*. This was originally the route of the railway from Parish's Pits to Ballast Wharf, and later of the railway from the Nordenfeldt Gun Co (which became Vickers) and Fraser & Chalmers. The route of the track-bed of both railways, which ran alongside each other, can be traced on the waste land just before West Street. Short sections of the old Vickers railway track can still be seen on both sides of the railway bridge.

Further along West Street note **The Trafalgar (17B)**, an interesting white pub; it is basically c1865, though the portico, ground floor bow windows, and upper floor bay windows were all added after 1900 to make it look like an earlier Regency pub.

18. *St John the Baptist Church. This flint and ragstone church, the original parish church of Erith, has a picturesque almost rural location, in a loop of the road, within a churchyard fringed by trees and crammed with monuments.

The church is low-lying with three parallel roofs of roughly similar size. Two cover the old church, consisting of the nave and chancel (which are 12th century) and the south aisle (which is 13th century); the north aisle was added during a restoration of 1877. At the west end of the nave is the tower, topped by a distinctive slender spire, probably 14th century.

> There was a church on the site in Saxon times, as Saxon work was found during the restoration of 1877. The nave and chancel of the present church were built in the 12th century, first the chancel c1100 and the nave later that century. The south aisle and chapel were added in the 13th century, the tower and spire probably in the 14th century. The south chapel was altered in the 15th century. The north aisle and vestry, and the south porch, were added during a substantial restoration by Habershon & Pite in 1877; the restoration also included rebuilding the tower, altering most of the windows into a late Gothic style, and renewing much of the walling.

On the south wall note, on a buttress to the right of the porch, a sundial of 1643. To its left an outline of a 13th century archway can be made out.

On the north wall the blocked Gothic doorway was introduced during the 1877 restoration. The lancet window above may have been repositioned from the original north wall.

The only windows not altered during the 1877 restoration are the lancet at the west end of the south aisle, the lancet above the west door of the tower and the three belfry lancets above, and the triple lancets of the chancel.

The entrance is via the south porch, which is of 1877. The **interior is highly interesting *(contact the Curate, 100 Park Crescent, 01322 332555, or Bob Knight, 17 Park Crescent Road, 01322 338507)*, particularly for two outstanding monuments and a collection of brasses which are among the finest in the London suburbs. It is crammed full of interesting furnishings and other details.

Inside the porch note the fine 13th century doorway with Purbeck marble shafts and lily capitals; note also before entering the magnificent 13th century oak door with its iron straps. Also in the porch is an old font, c1780.

Once inside, the two arcades are the dominant features - the south arcade is 13th century, and the north arcade was of course designed to match it in 1877. There are some prominent corbels, mostly grotesque, supporting some of the old roof timbers - in particular note the large grotesques on the south wall and on the northern side of the south arcade. Note also the strange creatures supporting the westernmost arches of the arcades.

Above the west door can be seen the outline of an early Gothic west doorway and of a window above, predating the construction of the tower. Note also the stones with a geometrical pattern around the doorway, visible inside the tower, which are probably 12th century and imported. There are also six stone coffin covers from Lesnes Abbey in the tower.

On the north aisle wall is a grand monument with a kneeling woman to Lord Eardley and his brother 1824, by Sir Francis Chantrey. In the window above is a fragment of medieval stained glass, representing the Agnus Dei. Both these were transferred from the chancel after the restoration. The pulpit at the east end of the aisle is elaborately Gothic, of 1877.

The walls of the chancel (which were originally exterior walls of the church) retain traces of several Norman arches, particularly around the eastern end where there was Norman arcading. To the left of the wide 13th century vestry arch to the north are a 16th century window opening and alongside a Norman window opening, and above are three 14th century clerestory openings. The east wall has three lancets, with postwar stained glass by Francis Spear, showing industrial and other local scenes. There are also two Norman window openings on either side of the wide chapel arch to the south. A tomb slab under the pews on the south side of the chancel covers the vault of Lord Eardley and family, including Maria Countess de Gersdorff.

On the floor by the vestry arch is the centrepiece of a reredos of 1877, elaborately carved with the Last Supper, placed here after the war. In the vestry is a classical hanging monument of 1826 to Maria Countess de Gersdorff (of the Eardley family), and below three panels (one around the fireplace) of floor tiles from Lesnes Abbey. Note also two small 19th century Doulton terracotta carvings by George Tinworth; and above some small stained glass panels which were from the original east window.

The most interesting features of the church are to be found in the south chapel, usually called the Wheatley Chapel because of the profusion of tablets and tomb-slabs to the Wheatley family, who were Lords of the Manor of Erith in the 18th and 19th centuries. The stained glass in the east window of the chapel is by C. E. Kempe 1905.

However, the two most outstanding monuments in the chapel are not to the Wheatley family, but to Elizabeth Countess of Shrewsbury 1568, in the south-east corner, and to Francis Vanacker 1686, in the north-east corner; both had been Lords of the Manor of Erith. The Shrewsbury monument is quite magnificent, with the effigy, her head pillow on a straw mat, lying on a classical tomb, with heraldic lozenges and other finely carved detail. The Vanacker monument consists of an elegant cartouche on the wall, and below a tomb-chest with marble top and beautifully carved sides, including a laurel-wreath, flowers and fruit, and three putti heads among clouds.

The brasses are all in the Wheatley Chapel, those on the floor being covered by floor mats; consult the location guide on the south wall. By the south wall are brass figures of John and Margery Ailemer 1435; and in the middle of the chapel under the chairs figures of John Mylner and wives (one missing) 1511. By the Shrewsbury monument is a tiny brass of three children, probably 16th century. By the Vanacker monument are brass figures of Roger Sencler 1425, and of Edward and Elizabeth Hawte 1537, with a tiny child below; under a niche above the monument is a small inscribed brass to Filice atte Cok, 13th century. By the altar is a brass figure of Emma Wode 1471, with a small armorial shield below. In a frame on the rood-screen is a brass fragment which is a palimpsest, inscribed both sides, one side probably c1380 and the other side to Anne Harman 1574.

Also in the Wheatley chapel is the entrance to the 15th century rood-loft stairs, and a 13th century archway on the south wall, which corresponds with the outline of the archway which can be discerned on the exterior. Note also two early medieval stone coffins, one from Lesnes Abbey.

The **churchyard** is attractive and interesting, though part to the rear will disappear with the pending construction of the Thamesmead to Erith Spine Road. The ornamental lych-gate is of 1885, and the stone wall of the churchyard of 1887. The two most prominent monuments are to James Harris 1752, large and classical, alongside the pathway to the porch, and to George & Anne Brown 1888, with typical Victorian decorative features, outside the east end. At the rear of the churchyard (due to be moved because of the road construction) is a tombstone to the Anderson family from 1860, including Sir William Anderson 1898, of Easton & Anderson, who was also Director General of the Royal Ordnance factories.

19. 33 Pembroke Road (19A) is an attractive late 19th century house, with round-headed windows and a strange bargeboarded gable.

20. Sandcliff Road connects with Nordenfeldt Road at the railway bridge under which ran the private railways of Parish's Pits, Vickers and Fraser & Chalmers *(see 17A).*

The industrial area here was the site of the Nordenfeldt Gun Works, set up in 1887, now part of the Europa Trading Estate *(see 23).* None of the earlier buildings can be seen properly from here.

At the junction with Church Road is a large industrial building with 19VSM06 (Vickers Son & Maxim 1906) on the gable ends; this was the Maxim gun factory.

ERITH - 47

21. *The Nordenfeldt. This imposing pub, known locally as the Pom Pom (after the machine gun made at the Vickers works nearby), is of 1902, though a section along Riverdale Road was originally a shop of 1898. Its design is symmetrical but quite extraordinary, and is best viewed from Pembroke Road opposite. Its rounded centre has an elaborate curved gable, and is flanked by turrets; from the apex the roof slopes sharply downwards on both sides.

22. The Old Tower Cinema, Fraser Road. A strange, almost harsh building. It started as a Primitive Methodist Chapel in 1901, and was converted in 1923 to become the Tower Cinema (hence the outline of a castellated tower on the upper floor). More recently it has been a meeting hall for Jehovah's Witnesses.

23. Europa Trading Estate, Fraser Road. This vast site occupies the area between Fraser Road and the railway line, taking up virtually the entire northern side of the road. It was originally a hilly site, and was used for quarrying from c1805, becoming known as Parish's Pits. Part of the site was acquired by Nordenfeldt in 1887, and a further part by Fraser & Chalmers in 1891. Fraser Road itself was laid out c1895, putting a southern limit to the site, though quarrying continued until 1971 from the area to the south known as Erith Quarry *(see 24)*.

Parish's Pits. Quarrying for stone ballast, sand and loam was started here by the Wheatley Estate c1805. After the break-up of the Estate in 1874, the quarry was taken over by the Parish family and it became known as Parish's Pits. At first the ballast was shipped from Lower Ballast Wharf (later called Railway Station Wharf); but from c1842 it was taken to Ballast Wharf (also known as Upper Ballast Wharf) by a private railway, crossed by a railway bridge when the main line opened in 1849. The site had been intensively quarried by the 1870s, and it was used as a recreation ground and cricket pitch; in fact, Australian test cricketers played local teams here in 1884 and in 1890.

Vickers. *(See also Crayford 7.)* In 1887 the Nordenfeldt Gun & Ammunition Co acquired the northern part of the site, accessible from Sandcliff Road. In 1888 the Maxim Company, making Sir Hiram Maxim's machine guns, which had moved to Crayford earlier that year, amalgamated with them to form the Maxim Nordenfeldt Gun & Ammunition Co. In 1897 they were purchased by Vickers and became Vickers Son & Maxim Ltd. Production of machine guns (known as the Pom Pom) continued, particularly during the Boer Wars, and by 1901 the works employed 4000 men. Private railways linked the site with Ballast Wharf and (going underneath Erith Station) with Railway Station Wharf *(see 27B)*.

In 1911 the name of the firm was changed to Vickers Ltd, and as well as increasing munitions production, the works commenced the manufacture of aircraft. Most early Vickers aircraft, from 1911 to 1914, were constructed at Erith, and were tested at Joyce Green Aerodrome on the Dartford Marshes. Vickers also had premises in Sandcliff Road *(see 20)*, Maxim Road and Corinthian Manor Way *(see 26)*.

After the war the Erith works was used for the production of various peacetime products. In 1927 Vickers amalgamated with Armstrongs to form Vickers Armstrong Ltd. and the manufacture of munitions resumed, but the Erith works closed in 1931 and production was transferred to Crayford.

Stone Vickers Warrior Works, off Church Manorway *(see Belvedere 29)*, is now the sole surviving part of the Vickers group in Erith or Crayford.

Fraser & Chalmers. In 1891 the American engineering firm of Fraser & Chalmers purchased part of the site from Maxim Nordenfeldt, and production of mining and milling machinery started in 1893. By 1908 it was manufacturing steam engines, and controlled the southern part of the site. GEC acquired Fraser & Chalmers in 1918, and expanded into other mechanical handling plant and electric furnaces. In 1937 the adjoining Vickers factory was purchased, and it then controlled nearly the whole site. GEC continued to use part of the site until the 1980s.

Several buildings used by Vickers and by Fraser & Chalmers in the 1900s have survived on the site.

Three main buildings (though much altered and extended) of Fraser & Chalmers from that period can be seen from Fraser Road. From the main entrance to the industrial estate, the large building to the left along the road was the Boiler Shop, and the large building ahead and to the left was the Foundry. From the western entrance gate, now barred, one can see a great brick-fronted steel-framed building with the date 1907 on the far left, which was the Turbine & Machine Shop.

The Vickers Son & Maxim buildings of the 1900s, which were at the rear, can only be seen from inside the site. *(Ask permission at the Estate Office to walk around the site.)* Walk past the Turbine & Machine Shop, and you come to a great complex of buildings on the right. These were the Vickers gun turnery, shell department, and gun mechanism department.

At the back of the site can be seen the remaining part of the quarried hill, forming a sort of 'sand-cliff', which was where quarrying stopped c1870. This gives some idea of how the site would have looked during quarrying. (There is a distant view of the 'sand-cliff' from the top of Fraser Road, near the junction with Bexley Road.)

In the part of the site now occupied by Cartwright Brice can be seen a large green screen against the railway embankment; this indicates the location of the tunnel under Erith Station for the railway siding which led directly from the site to Railway Station Wharf.

On the other side of Fraser Road is the derelict Atlas Paint & Chemicals works (at one stage associated with Denis Thatcher), opened 1929 and closed 1987.

24. Erith Quarry. This large area of waste land rising up south of Fraser Road and below Bexley Road contains the remaining parts of Parish's Pits, which were in use for quarrying until 1971. It is not accessible to the public, but a good idea of the site can be gained from Fraser Road.

A footpath, Birch Walk, runs alongside to the east, descending quite steeply from Bexley Road to Fraser Road; in parts the path is quite dramatic, running through a sort of ravine with Bexley Road looming above.

25. Hillside Estate, built by Doultons for its employees c1927, when the riverside works opened. The estate comprises Park Gardens, a close of five pairs off Valley Road, and 4/10 Pembroke Road, and are in an arts & crafts style with swooping roofs.

26. Corinthian Manorway. At the junction with West Street is a great dark brick structure, looking like a plinth for a disappeared statue; it actually contains a manhole, constructed in the 1920s for access to the Bedon stream which is culverted underneath on its way to the Thames about 200 metres away.

Further along, disused railway siding track crosses the road; it linked the Vickers munitions works, which opened here c1912, with the Vickers gun carriage works at Maxim Road.

27. Riverside Walk. This runs between Corinthian Manorway and Riverside Gardens, and gives good views across the river to Coldharbour Point and Rainham Marshes. However, sections of the walk are not always very pleasant, and landward views are mostly blocked by concrete walling.

Starting from Corinthian Manorway, you soon come to a long modern pier, which is in use for private boats. Around are wharves once used by Erith Gas Works, set up by West Kent Gas Company in 1862 and closed c1914 *(see Crayford 20)*, and then used by the Vickers gun carriage works in Maxim Road.

You then come to **Ballast Wharf (27A)**, also known as Upper Ballast Wharf, with derelict jetties and a dock; it was first constructed 1842 to take ballast and loam from Parish's Pits and remained in use for ballast until 1971. It was also used by Vickers and by Fraser & Chalmers. From the dock a footpath leads to West Street.

Just before Riverside Gardens, one comes to the dock of **Railway Station Wharf (27B)**, formerly called Lower Ballast Wharf, used for shipping ballast from Parish's Pits between 1808 and 1842. Later it was used by Vickers and by Fraser & Chalmers. Its use ceased in the 1930s.

ERITH

Gazetteer

Section 'D' NORTHUMBERLAND HEATH
(See map on page 38)

28. Our Lady of the Angels Church, Bexley Road. A grand and imposing red brick Roman Catholic church of 1963. The bulky campanile tapers up to an open belfry, the open portico has three tall archways, and there is a series of round-headed windows along both sides.

The **interior** *(call at the Friary next door, or telephone 01322 33193 beforehand)* is bright and spacious; there are two stained glass windows of St Francis and St Clare which were transferred from the previous Roman Catholic church of 1870 in West Street, demolished in 1989.

The church is linked to the **Franciscan Friary** (of the Capuchin Fathers) of 1903, large and rather solemn-looking with a Gothic entrance.

29. Erith Cemetery, with sites on both sides of Brook Street. The eastern side was opened in 1894, and its elevated site provides fantastic sweeping views to the north. Just beyond the entrance is a cross commemorating '7 of the 13 who lost their lives in a disastrous explosion at Slade Green 1924'. (The explosion was on the premises of W. V. Gilbert, which adjoined Thames Ammunition Works on Crayford Marshes.) Note the central chapel of 1894, with its strange central bell-tower. The western side was opened after the last war.

30. The Duchess of Kent, Brook Street. An attractive and jolly pub of 1905 in a vaguely Arts & Crafts style, with a pretty corner oriel topped by a conical roof.

31. Northumberland Heath School, erected by the Erith School Board in 1895. It has four great gables along the frontage, with a distinctive blue-topped tower in the middle, and lots of decorative detail. The similar building behind is of 1901. To the north is the Northumberland Heath Evening Centre, red brick, of 1932.

32. St Pauls Church, Mill Road. The parish church of Northumberland Heath. A rather dull and bulky red brick Gothic church of 1901, with a quirky conical bellcote. It is oriented to the north; the baptistry was added in 1905.

The **interior** *(contact 01322 332809)* is impressive and lofty, with a bold Gothic arcade and elongated windows in the apse. The stained glass windows in the baptistry are of 1880, having been transferred from the original mission church of 1874, which was until 1962 alongside on the site of the present church hall.

33. In St Pauls Road is part of the circular brick **base** of an early 19th century smock **windmill**, which was in use until c1880. It can be seen along a lane on the east side of the road, but a better view can be obtained from the car park of Wellingtons Service Centre, 46 Mill Road. *Ask at Wellingtons for permission to view.* Wellingtons was the original mill-house, converted and with a modern frontage.

34. 25 Mill Road, an imposing house, probably of the 1870s, with fanciful bargeboarded gables and an odd portico.

35. Belmont Snooker Club, Belmont Road, retains the Gothic arched entrance porch of the school-house of University Place School of 1865-70; the rest of the building was totally transformed in the early 1980s.

36. Belmont House, 125 Belmont Road, a fine mid 19th century white house with a handsome portico.

37. The Brewers Arms, 22 Brook Street. An attractive pub of the mid 1860s, the ground floor covered with pretty Trumans green tiling c1910.

38. The Duke of Northumberland. This pub, basically of the mid 1860s, heralds the approach to Northumberland Heath from the south. The original entrance was at the corner facing the road junction.

39. Northumberland Heath Estate. The estate was designed by Gordon Allen and built 1915-16 by Vickers to house munitions workers. It extends in a wide arc from Erith Road to Colyers Lane, centred on Barnehurst Avenue, and also including Heath Way and Northumberland Way. The house styles are similar to those at Barnes Cray Garden Village *(see Crayford 44)*; and good groups can be seen at Barnehurst Close, 29/43 Barnehurst Avenue, and 416/426 Erith Road, an attractive semi-circular group around a green on the roundabout. Many houses have been altered and there is much later infill.

ERITH

Suggested Walks

It is recommended that the suggested walks be followed in conjunction with the Gazetteer and the map (on page 38), and that the Gazetteer be consulted at each location for a detailed description. Most locations described in Section 'A' and all locations in Sections 'B' & 'C' are included. The walks follow a more or less circular route, so can be joined at any location. Section 'D' is not covered; the locations are not numerous, and most are closely concentrated and it is not necessary to suggest a route. The walks begin and end at Erith Station.

WALK No 1 (including Erith High Street, the Town Centre, Lesney Park Estate, and Christ Church). Distance approx four kilometres.

NB. Erith Museum is open Monday, Wednesday and Saturday afternoons. Erith Market operates Wednesdays and Saturdays. Try to make an advance arrangement - see the gazetteer - to see the interior of Christ Church.

SECTION 'A'. On leaving **Erith Station (1)**, bear right up to the roundabout; note **Erith Town Hall (2)** opposite. Turn left down Walnut Tree Road, noting **Erith Library (3)** (visit **Erith Museum** inside if possible), the former **Electricity Generating Station**, and **Riverside Swimming Centre (4)**, all on the right-hand side. Bear right for the **Riverside Gardens (5)**; note the **Running Horses** pub, and at the end of the gardens, go down to the river for the view and return, then turn left.

You are now in **Erith High Street (6)**; on the left is a sequence of interesting buildings - the **Police Station, Stone Court, The Cross Keys, Erith Playhouse,** and **The White Hart**. Ahead is the **Town Centre (7)**, with **Town Square** and the open air **Erith Market** on the right; from the market take the path through to **Queen Street Baptist Church (8)**.

Walk down Queen Street to the High Street; note **Mecca Bingo Club** opposite. Turn left and right into Pier Road, noting **Bank Chambers** on the right. Ahead is **Erith Deep Wharf (9)**, unused and with no public access. Bear right into Avenue Road, noting **Erith Trades & Social Club** on the left. At the roundabout, **Manor Road (10)** is to the left; walk along it, depending on the time you have, and return. Continue along Avenue Road, cross the main road and the bridge over the railway.

SECTION 'B'. You are now in the residential part of **Avenue Road (12)**. Continue and turn right along Victoria Road, which brings you into the main part of the **Lesney Park Estate (14)**. Continue, noting **76/78 Park Crescent (14C)** to the left, to **Christ Church (13)**; try to see the interior.

ERITH- 53

Return along Victoria Road to **Lesney Park Road**, and turn right. Note **nos 1/3 (14A), nos 5 & 7**, and further along, **Hainault (14B)**, all on the left. At the end, turn right into **Lesney Park**, and note **no 83** on the left. Turn left into **Park Crescent**; take the short lane to the left to see **no 173 (14D)**. Continue along Park Crescent, noting **no 226 (14E)** on the right and **Erith Hospital (15)** on the left, until you emerge on Bexley Road.
SECTION 'D'. Note opposite **Our Lady of the Angels Church (28)** and the **Franciscan Friary**.
SECTION 'B'. Turn right down **Bexley Road (16)**, noting **St Marys (16C)** and **no 88 (16B)** on the left and **nos 63/65 (16A)** on the right, until you reach the roundabout, then bear left for the Station.

WALK No 2 (including West Street, St John the Baptist Church, Europa Industrial Estate and the riverside walk). Distance approx four kilometres.
It is worth trying to make an advance arrangement - see the gazetteer - to view the interior of St John the Baptist Church.
SECTION 'C'. On leaving **Erith Station (1)**, proceed straight ahead down Stonewood Road, and turn left into **West Street (17)**. Continue along West Street, noting **Nordenfeldt Road (17A)** and then **The Trafalgar (17B)** on the left, until you reach **St John the Baptist Church (18)**; try to see the interior.
Leave through the lych-gate, turn right and cross the railway bridge into **Pembroke Road**. Note **no 33 (19)** on the left, and the old Maxim gun factory round the corner in **Sandcliff Road (20)**. At the end of Pembroke Road is **The Nordenfeldt (21)**, and to its left, the **old Tower Cinema (22)**. Bear left along Fraser Road until you reach the first (barred) entrance to the **Europa Trading Estate (23)**. From here you can see the Fraser & Chalmers Turbine & Machine Shop. (If you wish to see the rest of the site, continue to the main entrance and ask permission at the Estate Office.) **Erith Quarry (24)** is opposite.
Return and walk down Pembroke Road. Off Valley Road to the left is the **Hillside Estate (25)**. Cross the railway bridge and continue to the road junction by the churchyard. If you have time, it is worth turning left along Lower Road then right into Church Manorway *(see Belvedere 29)* to see the industrial premises. Cross from the churchyard into **Corinthian Manorway (26)**, and turn right along the **Riverside Walk (27)**. At the end, by Riverside Gardens, cross the road into Stonewood Road and back to the Station.

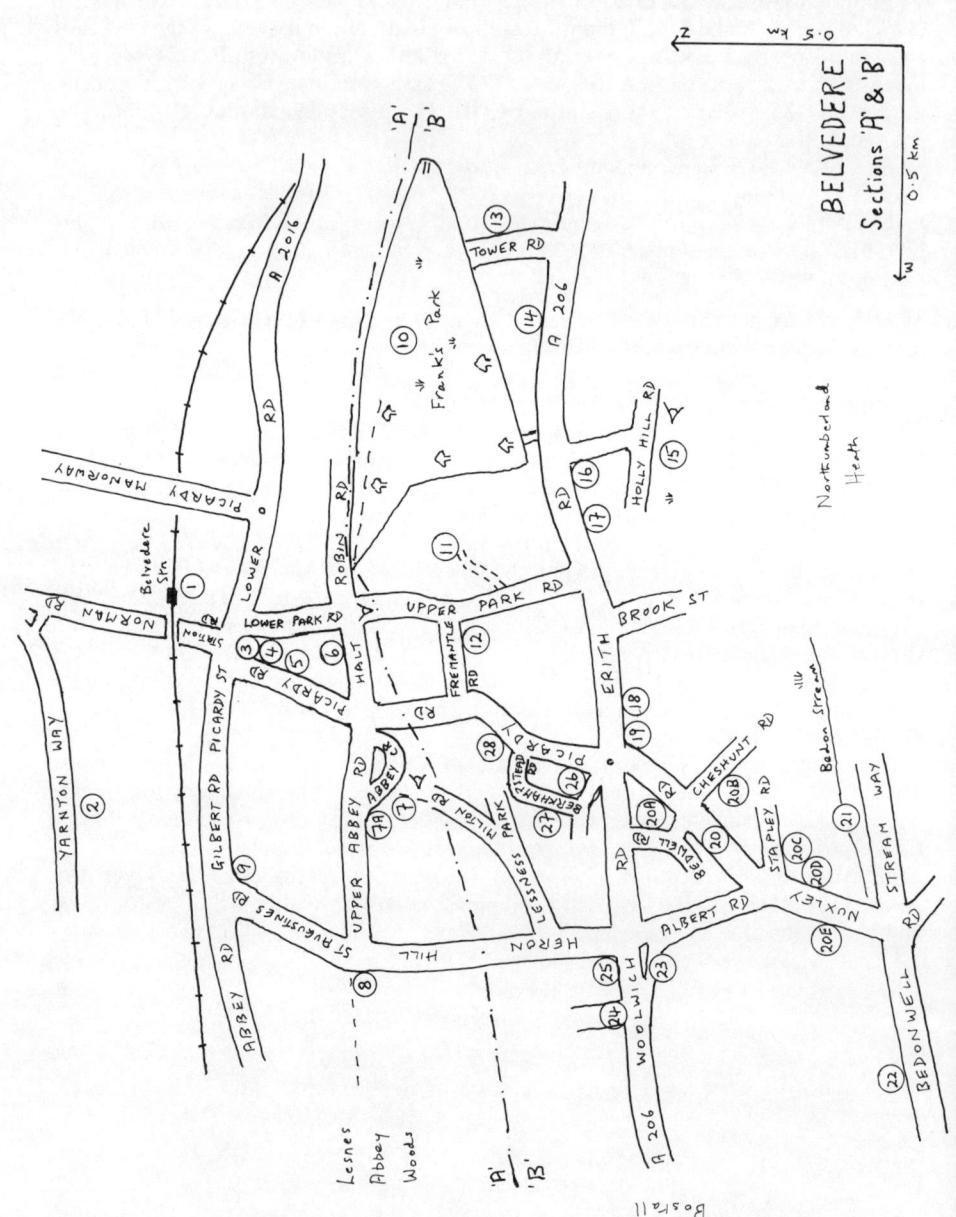

BELVEDERE

Gazetteer

Section 'A' LOWER BELVEDERE

1. Belvedere Station. Originally opened in 1859; the present very basic building is of 1968. The grass strip alongside the down track is the track-bed of the old siding to Belvedere Gas Works.

2. Belvedere Gas Works. It was set up by the South Suburban Gas Company c1922 as a gas holder station. The two gas holders are of 1923 and of 1931. *(See also Crayford 20.)*

3. The Belvedere. A really handsome classical pub with a portico, c1860.

4. 13/15 Lower Park Road, three distinctive large houses of the 1860s. The main entrances are on Lower Park Road, but they also have entrances on Picardy Road, each entrance having a different address. The houses are, going from south to north: 13 Lower Park Road / 10 Picardy Road, classical; 14 Lower Park Road / 8 Picardy Road, with a Tudor porch; and 15 Lower Park Road / 6 Picardy Road, with prominent gables on both sides.

5. Belvedere Methodist Church, Picardy Road, a striking Gothic church of 1876, with a fine Gothic porch and a wheel-window above.

6. 5/8 Halt Robin Road, two impressive pairs of the 1860s with pediments and round-headed windows. Nos 7/8 retain a rusticated ground floor.

7. *Milton Road and Abbey Crescent form a wonderful townscape as they descend the hill; the houses are on the west side, and provide fantastic views eastwards towards the river. Milton Road descends from a small green, and then becomes a flight of steps with terraced houses directly on the steps leading down to Abbey Crescent, where a terrace continues curving to the west and rounding the corner with the pub **Prince Alfred (7A)**. Abbey Crescent is probably of the 1860s, Milton Road probably of the 1870s, and the Prince Alfred probably c1870.

8. *The Old Leather Bottle, Heron Hill. A highly attractive late 18th century pub, the ground floor altered and a small east extension added in the early 19th century. It may contain structure dating back to 1643.

9. Church of St Augustine, Gilbert Road. A large red brick romanesque church by Temple Moore of 1916, the present west front and porch added 1962. It has lots of romanesque features, including a clerestory of round-headed windows and, at the east end, an apse and gable with Lombard arches. The **interior** *(contact the Vicarage, St Augustines Road, 0181-311 6307)* is very imposing, with great round red brick arches. The church hall projects as an extension to the south.

BELVEDERE

Gazetteer

Section 'B' UPPER BELVEDERE
(See map on page 54)

10. *Frank's Park. Originally part of the grounds of Belvedere House, it became a public park when acquired by Erith Council in 1920. It was named after Frank Beadle, a local industrialist living at The Oaks *(see 14)*, who bequeathed the money for the purchase; a pillar near the children's playground commemorates the bequest, but its plaque has disappeared.

The park is highly attractive, with a flat grassed area surrounded (except to the east) by a horseshoe of precipitous hills. The hills are densely wooded, with magnificent oak, sweet chestnut and beech trees; they form the eastern point of the ridge which runs from Bostall Heath through Lesnes Abbey Wood and Upper Belvedere.

On top of a hill in the northern part of the park is a sunken concrete bowl, the remains of a garden feature belonging to Temple Mount, a mid 19th century house, demolished after the last war, which was on the hill.

11. Heathdene Drive. The houses at the eastern end of this road occupy the site of **Belvedere House**.

> The original Belvedere House was built c1740, and in 1751 it was acquired by Sampson Gideon, a City financier. He died in 1763, and in 1764 James 'Athenian' Stuart rebuilt the house for his son Sir Sampson Gideon, later to become Lord Eardley.
>
> In 1847 the estate was inherited by Sir Culling Eardley; he built All Saints Church in 1853 and developed the Belvedere Estate outside the grounds from 1859, and was thus largely responsible for the development of the area of Belvedere. He died in 1863, and the mansion was sold in 1865 to the Shipwrecked Mariners Society, and later became known as the Royal Alfred Home for Aged Seamen.
>
> In 1920 the eastern part of the grounds became Frank's Park. In 1959 the old mansion was replaced by a large modern block, but this was in turn demolished in 1978. The site, and the western part of the grounds, were developed for housing in the early 1980s.

12. 5 Fremantle Road was the lodge for The Manor, a large late 19th century house, now demolished, which had become the infirmary for the seamen's home.

13. Bexley College, Tower Road. This is the main site of Bexley College, formerly the Erith College of Technology. As one enters the campus, to the left is the workshop block of 1966 and to the right the main admin block of 1971, a bulky tower block set inside a concrete frame. In front of the latter is the Library, notable for the sharply swept down corners of its roof.

14. Trinity School, Erith Road. The lodge at the entrance to the school was the lodge for The Oaks, a building probably of the 1870s (the residence of Frank Beadle, *see 10*). It was demolished in the 1970s when the school was built.

15. Holly Hill, a large open space on a hilltop, with magnificent views over Erith and the riverside. It was the site of Holly Hill House, built c1860, demolished c1947.

16. Erith Road Campus of Bexley College, originally known as Erith Technical Institute and subsequently the original building of the Erith College of Technology. A magnificent building of 1906, with a prominent turret and octagonal cupola, lavish use of terracotta, and lots of ornamental flourishes.

Nearby at 47 Erith Road is **Redcliffe Campus**, also part of Bexley College, a grand house with a magnificent bargeboarded gable, probably c1905.

17. 37/45 Erith Road, an unusual terrace, probably c1905, with doorways flanked by bulbous columns, pointed oriels, and other interesting decorative features.

18. The Laurels, 7 Erith Road. An attractive house of the 1860s, with a tower and a long parapetted first floor terrace.

19. All Saints Church. A Victorian Gothic flint church, looking like an elongated village church. Prominent features are the tower with its shingled spire, the long north transept with its triple dormers, and similar single dormers on the south transept and on each side of the nave roof. The nave and chancel were built 1853 by William & Edward Habershon as a proprietary chapel for Sir Culling Eardley, and the tower added in 1861 when it became the original parish church of Belvedere. The transepts were added in 1864, when the church assumed its present appearance.

The ***interior** *(contact the Vicarage next door, phone 01322 432169)* is long and striking when viewed from the west door, and eccentric when one looks at the details. The nave arcades continue straight past the transepts and up to the chancel. The transepts have galleries, with extraordinary curved balcony fronts of cast-iron foliage; there is a large rose window above the north gallery, and the south gallery is taken up by the organ. The fine hammerbeam roof rests on fantastic carved and vividly painted corbels, including some grotesque heads. The reredos is lavishly decorated. On the east wall of the north transept are tablets to Isabella Lady Eardley 1860 and Sir Culling Eardley 1863, commemorating their role in the foundation of the church.

20. Nuxley Road is a minor shopping centre, and retains a village atmosphere, with several older buildings, though some have been quite drastically altered. Note, from north to south:

The **Vicarage** of 1853, adjacent to the church, with fanciful bargeboards over the porch and gables. Later extension to the south, and contemporary coach-house.

6 Bedwell Road (20A), similar to the Vicarage, with fanciful bargeboarded porch and gables, probably of the 1860s.

4/12 Cheshunt Road (20B), a terrace of cottages of the 1860s, with quaint dormers and Gothic windows.

Belvedere Social Club, 27/37 Nuxley Road, originally a unified terrace of the 1860s, but much altered. Note the series of different sized gables, and the Gothic door and windows in the northern block.

45 Nuxley Road, formerly called the Coffee Tavern, now a restaurant, late 19th century, though it looks like an older cottage.

18/20 Stapley Road (20C), two houses set back from the road, probably early 19th century, and the oldest surviving houses in Belvedere.

The Fox, an attractive and bold pub, basically of 1853 but refronted 1921.

Free Grace Baptist Chapel (20D), a simple classical building opened as a strict chapel in 1805; no 83 adjoining is probably mid 19th century. (Ask permission at no 83 to see the **interior**, which is small and pleasing, with a gallery.)

The Queens Head (20E), with the adjoining shop no 106, of 1871. Note the masks along the upper floor of both pub and shop.

21. **Stream Way**. This street borders an attractive area of open space around the Bedon stream, and further east it opens out into a parkland area with real rural atmosphere. A footpath leads down from Grosvenor Road to a bridge over the stream. This is the only place where the Bedon stream can be seen; from here it is culverted underground to the Thames at Corinthian Manorway.

22. **306/320 Bedonwell Road.** Two adjacent groups of farmworkers houses c1894, impressive, each group having fine end gables.

23. **Belvedere Green.** This small triangular green, which has survived from Lessness Heath, is a focal point and gives a village atmosphere to Upper Belvedere. It is continued further west by a narrower green with a line of trees.

Overlooking the Green, on the corner with Albert Road, is the pub **The Prince of Wales**, probably of 1863.

Further along, **33/45 Woolwich Road** form an interesting group; note in particular no 33, a fine Italianate house of 1879, and nos 43/45, large and distinguished, c1862.

24. **50/64 Woolwich Road**, four attractive and dignified pairs of the 1860s. Interrupting the group is **Gloucester Road**, where nos 1/3, 9/11, 2/4 and 6/8 survive from the same period. Many houses have been very much altered.

25. **The Eardley Arms**, an attractive pub with nice decorative details; it is of the 1860s, on the site of an inn of 1789. Over the corner doorway is the coat of arms of the Eardley family, who owned Belvedere House *(see 11).* The building to the right has been converted from the village smithy.

26. **163/169 Picardy Road**, an interesting group of houses. First, at the junction with Woolwich Road, is **The Priory**, no 169, a very large house of 1866, with bargeboarded porch and Gothic doorways. The bargeboarded coach-house to the right is contemporary. The archaeologist Flaxman Spurrell lived here in the 1880s.

Nos 165/7 is an imposing Italianate pair, of the 1860s.

Chilton Lodge, no 163, also of the 1860s, is white and fanciful, with a central tower and a bargeboarded porch with a Gothic doorway.

27. **Heathfield**, 14 Berkhampstead Road. An impressive detached Italianate villa, the only survivor of a development of the 1860s along Berkhampstead Road and Essenden Road.

28. **Belvedere & Erith Congregational Church**, Picardy Road. Built 1897, it has an intricately patterned Gothic frontage.

BELVEDERE

Gazetteer

Section 'C' RIVERSIDE INDUSTRIAL ZONE
(See map on page 60)

29. Church Manorway. This road is lined by industrial premises still in operation.
   First, on the right, is the British Gypsum site; the tracks of an old rail siding to the site from the main line east of Belvedere Station can be seen crossing the road.
   Next you come to the piers of a railway bridge, partly hidden by trees and shrubs, which used to form part of the siding to Erith Oil Works.
   Erith Oil Works *(see 30)* is now on the right, and over to the left is the Stone Vickers Warrior Works, the sole surviving Vickers site in either Erith or Crayford.
   Beyond, to the left, is the BICC site *(see 31)*, with its imposing cable cooling tower, and on the right, the War Memorial and Garden of Remembrance, unveiled 1923, to BICC employees who lost their lives in the First World War. The large area of waste land beyond was the BICC sports ground.
   At the end is the United Marine Aggregates site.

30. *Erith Oil Works. Part of ADM (Archer Daniels Midland) Ltd since 1990; beforehand the works was called British Oil & Cake Mills, and was part of Unilever. It processes rape-seed oil for human consumption, with the residue being used as animal feed, and is the largest works of its kind in the country.
   Note the bank of 24 concrete cylindrical silos, tightly packed together in four rows of six, carried on slim concrete pilotis, and topped by a wide roof of three wavey pediments. They were constructed in 1916, the first major work in Britain using the reinforced concrete techniques pioneered in Denmark by Christiani & Nielsen.
   Other substantial buildings, of brick with tall pilasters, remain from the early factory. They include, to the left of the silos, mills of 1915 linked by a bridge, and behind, the original office building inscribed 1908 EOW 1914.
   Behind the old silos, clearly visible from the Riverside Walk *(see 33)*, are a stack of four concrete cylinders of 1978, slim and tall; and a large silo with a pyramidal top c1976 supported on squat pilotis. The factory has a substantial jetty on the river, and nearby is a large red brick tank-house of 1922, with some nice decorative features.

31. BICC (British Insulated Callenders Cables). This factory covers a vast area between Church Manorway and Crabtree Manorway. It is dominated by the spectacular *cable cooling tower of 1992, 75 metres high, crisp and rectangular.
   From the main entrance in Church Manorway, the factory seems largely modern. However, the five sheds, parallel with the road, on the extreme right of the premises are basically cable sheds c1902, recently modernised and converted with new roofs.

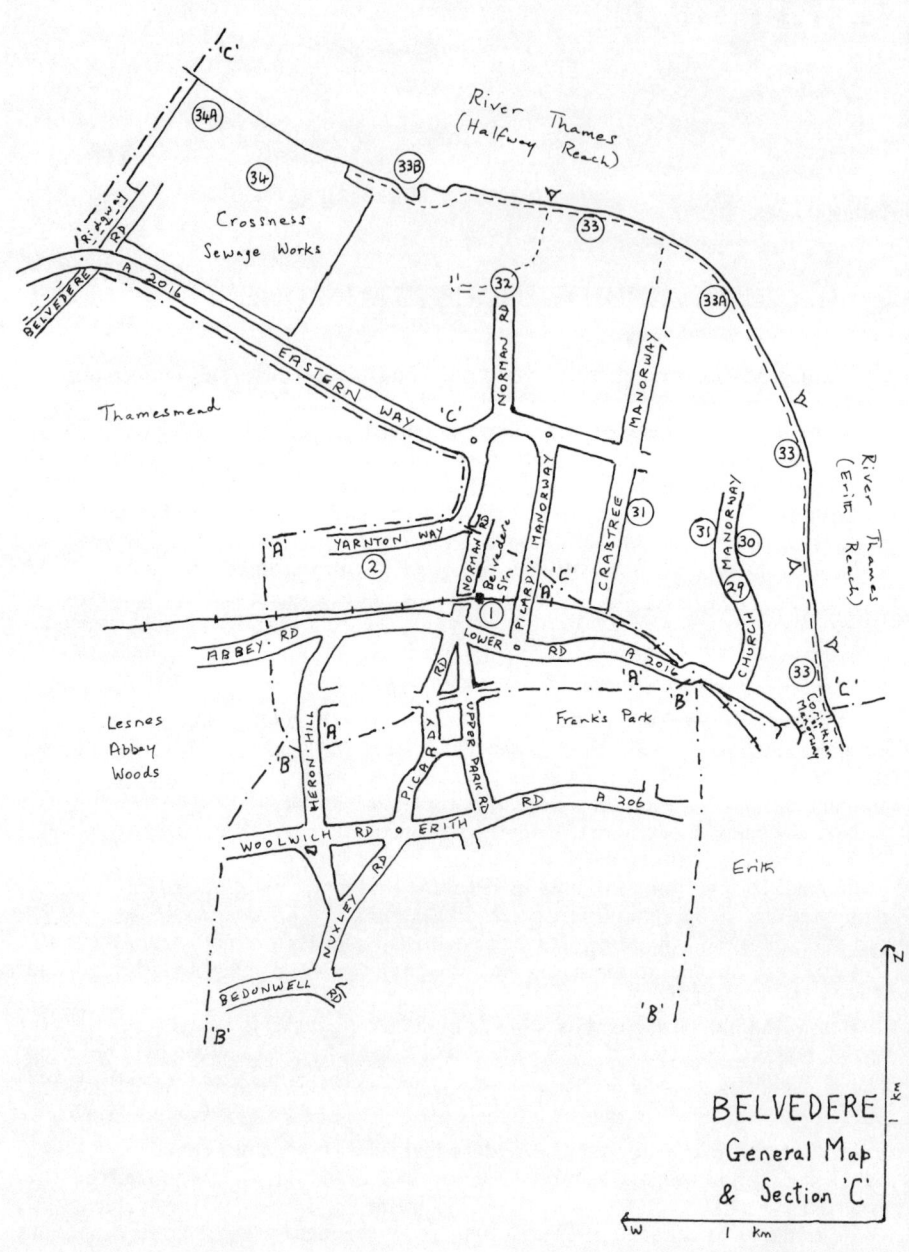

From the entrance in Crabtree Manorway, the sheds on the left (now used by Helio Mirror Co) were BICC sheds of 1917, set up to produce field telephone cable for trench warfare in the first world war; the white sheds straight ahead, with their distinctive protruding air vents, are of 1938.
(For the War Memorial and the old sports ground, see 29.)

Callender & Sons was founded for the import and use of bitumen by William Ormiston Callender in 1877, and moved to their first major works here in 1880. In 1882 it became the Callender Bitumen, Telegraph and Waterproof Co. Manufacture of cables was at first a sideline to bitumen products, but it soon became the factory's main activity. In 1896 it was reorganised as the Callender Cable and Construction Co, later changed to British Insulated Callenders Cables. Sir Tom Callender, son of the founder, who lived at 115 Woolwich Road *(see Abbey Wood 13)*, was the main director and the moving force from 1896 until the 1930s. By 1965 the site here was the principal manufacturing unit of the world's largest cable group.

BICC manufactured much of the cable for PLUTO (Pipe line under the ocean) in the preparations for the D-Day landings in 1944. The cable was loaded into specially converted cable-laying ships tied up at the jetty of the neighbouring Erith Oil Works.

32. Norman Road. To the right of the road, and extending to the river, was the site of the Belvedere Power Station, built in 1962; it was considered an outstanding industrial monument, but was largely demolished in 1993. The building on the left is Belvedere Sub-Station, a long rectangular building, the only remaining part of the Power Station complex still in use. On the main site itself, nearer the river, the only buildings remaining are stores, workshops and office buildings.

Straight ahead at the end of the road is the site of the Borax refinery, which operated from 1899 to 1993; on and around here is the proposed location for the Cory waste-to-energy incinerator, which if it proceeds would be the largest in the world. A road to the left leads to the Fords car park, linked to the jetty for Fords ferry-boats crossing to the Dagenham works opposite *(see 33)*.

33. *Riverside Walk, extending from Corinthian Manorway to Crossness Sewage Works, a distance of over 3 kilometres. The pathway throughout is quite broad and well paved, mostly concrete (constructed in the 1970s as part of the Thames flood defences); though there is quite a steep hump when passing the Erith Oil Works site. There are fine views over the river wall (except for short sections where it is too high) and over the industrial sites inland, and in parts the atmosphere is quite evocative. Parallel inland is the great wooded ridge from Frank's Park through Lesnes Abbey Woods to Bostall Heath, and beyond is Shooters Hill.

The walk can be accessed readily at two points only - by footpaths at the end of Corinthian Manorway, and at the end of Crabtree Manorway. (There is another access by turning right at the end of the straight stretch of Norman Road, between the old Power Station and the Borax sites, but this is unpleasant and not to be recommended.) The walk is described in two sections, from Corinthian Manorway to Crabtree Manorway, and from Crabtree Manorway to the Crossness Sewage Works; in both cases, retracing steps to the starting-point cannot be avoided.

(i) Corinthian Manorway to Crabtree Manorway. This section passes industrial sites which are still largely in use.

First you come to a T jetty of British Gypsum with a conveyor above the path; and then a disused grass-covered jetty, which belonged to Doulton, which made stoneware pipes etc from c1927 to 1974.

Next is the very large jetty of Erith Oil Works *(see 30)*, with its impressive silos. Then you come to the old BICC sports ground, with the BICC works, dominated by its cable cooling tower *(see 31)*, beyond. At this point are some derelict BICC jetties, with a conveyor crossing above them to a jetty of United Marine Aggregates.

The next jetty is of Redland Aggregates. Beyond is the disused shipping beacon at **Jenningtree Point (33A)**, where there is an open meadow, and the footpath leading to Crabtree Manorway.

(ii) Crabtree Manorway to Crossness Sewage Works. This section passes a series of largely derelict industrial sites before reaching the Crossness Works.

First you come to the long derelict jetty, parallel to the path, of Burt, Boulton & Haywood, a timber firm still operating at the end of Crabtree Manorway.

Next is a large jetty with a bridge over the path, which was used by Belvedere Power Station *(see 32)*.

At this point, between the Power Station and the Borax sites, is the footpath from Norman Road *(see above)*. The next two sites are also derelict - Borax, with two smaller jetties and old internal rail tracks crossing the path; and Rentons, with its jetty and timber storage shed still there.

The final jetty before Crossness, and the only jetty in this section still in use, is owned by Fords and used by their ferry-boats to take employees using the staff car park nearby across to their Dagenham works.

The path now turns inland at **Halfway Reach Bay (33B)**, where there are reedbeds and saltmarshes between the path and the river, and you come to the Crossness Sewage Works *(see 34)*. At first you continue alongside an unused part of the site, and then you come to a great fence with the outfall just beyond, and a notice saying 'Thames Water warning - outfall apron extends 50 metres from this board'; this is where the operational part of the site begins, and one can see the jetty of the Sludge Booster Station (where untreated sludge is loaded for dumping at sea, pending construction of incinerators by 1998).

34. Crossness Sewage Treatment Works, Belvedere Road. This modern establishment of 1964 covers a vast riverside area at the end of the **Southern Outfall Sewer**, which was constructed in 1862 as part of the comprehensive London sewage system created 1860-65 by Sir Joseph Bazalgette, chief engineer of the Metropolitan Board of Works. The only access to the Sewage Works is by Belvedere Road, Thamesmead South.

The sewer (which actually consists of three brick-lined outfall sewers, one the original high-level, the other two low-level of 1909) begins at the Greenwich Sewage Pumping Station, Greenwich High Road, where sewage from many points in South London is pumped up 6 metres. Through Plumstead, Abbey Wood and Thamesmead, the sewer runs, with the sewage flowing by gravity, within an immense grassy embankment, and a footpath runs along the top of the embankment.

The footpath, known as **Ridgway**, is at present being improved and will then be open to the public. Access will be from several points, in Nathan Way and White Hart Road in Plumstead, Sewell Road in Abbey Wood, and Belvedere Road in Thamesmead.

The building on the left just beyond the entrance gate is the Screen House, where large objects are removed before the sewage goes on for treatment; this is in effect where the sewers end. (This is the only building of the modern works visible from outside, though the sludge jetty and the outfall itself can be seen from the western end of the Riverside Walk in Belvedere - see 33.)

The area of the modern works also embraces the *old works (34A), an impressive complex of buildings, all in an Italian romanesque style. Work has been under way since 1985 by the Crossness Engines Trust (a voluntary body) on a long-term project of restoring the old works, to become a heritage museum concentrating on steam and public health, with access through Thamesmead North. In the meantime there are normally open days during the year, otherwise special arrangements have to be made for viewing the works - see below. The only good view of the old works from outside the site is from the footpath beyond the Riverside Golf Course in Thamesmead (see Thamesmead 22A).

The main building is Bazalgette's **Beam Engine House** of 1865, which contains the finest group of old beam engines in the world. The House is a large Italian palazzo in romanesque style, with quite fantastic decorative brickwork, archways with dogtooth ornamentation, corbel blocks, Portland stone columns and capitals. There was originally a mansard roof, replaced by the present flat roof in 1927.

The ****interior** has extraordinary elaborate cast iron work, particularly in the galleries and in the pillars and screens of the central octagonal shaft.

The octagon (consisting of four screens and four archways) was a decorative architectural feature, and also formed a light-well; one screen has now been restored in original colours, and work has started on other screens and archways. Each screen has the monogram MBW (Metropolitan Board of Works).

There are four massive rotative beam engines (each beam 12.8 metres long), built by James Watt & Co of Birmingham, probably the largest such engines ever constructed and certainly the largest surviving in Europe. The beam engines were named 'Victoria', 'Prince Consort', 'Albert Edward' and 'Alexandra'. It is hoped that by 1997 'Prince Consort' will be restored, and will be in working order by the Millennium. The engines were used for pumping sewage into reservoirs before discharge into the river at the ebb tide; they have not been in use since 1953, nor in regular use since 1914.

Attached to the engine house are, to the south, the boiler house of 1865, and to the north, the triple-expansion engine house, the construction of which in 1899 enclosed the original entrance archway. Access to the engine house is now through the boiler house.

On entering the engine house, note on the right the main penstock rams, which controlled the sluices regulating the flow of sewage to a duct beneath the floor. Also note nearby the connecting rods for the enormous sewage pumps below, two of which are linked to each of the beam engines above; and the great 8.5 metres diameter flywheels. Walk through the north doorway into the triple-expansion house to see the original grand romanesque entrance archway with its chevron and dogtooth decoration; the archway is not otherwise visible from outside.

Climb the staircase to see the triple-expansion cylinders at an intermediate level, and the actual beams at the top level. It is possible to descend a staircase to the basement to see one of the pumps in its great barrel.

On either side of the boiler house are two single storey buildings of 1865 - to the east the fitting shop, and to the west the 'garage' (formerly used as a shed for the site tramway, and as an apprentices school). The pond near the river is the sole survivor of a number of cooling ponds on the site.

To the east of the complex is the Centrifugal Engine House, a building of 1914; it contains electric pumps used for storm sewage, and is the only old building still in use by the Sewage Works. Further east, parallel with the river, are the Precipitation Works of 1891, a large building with the boiler house to the north and engine house to the south. All these buildings are in the same impressive architectural style as the old Beam Engine House, with much decorative detail.

To the south of the old works, and under a large grassed area, are the storm tanks of the modern works, which have been converted from the original underground reservoirs of 1869. (There is a view over this grassed area from the terrace in front of the boiler house, within the Old Works complex.) The old ramps which led down into the reservoirs can be seen at the south end of this area, and opposite this is a large lake and the administration building for the modern works. The installations of the modern works lie to the east of this building.

There is normally no access to the Old Works for individuals. However, open days are arranged on a Saturday and/or a Sunday in the spring and in the summer, and additionally visits can be made by appointment only on one Tuesday and one Sunday in each month. Ring officers of the Crossness Engines Trust - Michael Dunmow on 0181-303 6723, or John Ridley on 01322 522937 - to check when visits may be possible. Leaflets containing more technical descriptions of the Works can be obtained on such occasions.

Visits to the modern works are also interesting, and Thames Water sometimes arranges visits for groups. Ring 0181-310 1116 to enquire whether it is possible to join a party visiting the modern works.

BELVEDERE

Suggested Walks

It is recommended that the suggested walks be followed in conjunction with the Gazetteer and the map (on page 54), and that the Gazetteer be consulted at each location for a detailed description. All locations in Section 'A' and most locations in Section 'B' are included; some locations in Section 'B' are not included, as they might add too much to the length of the walks. Section 'C' is not covered, as the locations are best viewed from the Riverside Walk, which is described in the gazetteer; the Crossness Sewage Works needs a separate visit on an open day - see the gazetteer. The walks follows a more or less circular route, so can be joined at any location. The walks begin and end at Belvedere Station.

WALK No 1 (covering Lower Belvedere). Distance approx two kilometres.

NB. Try to make an advance arrangement - see the gazetteer - to see the interior of St Augustines Church.

SECTION 'A'. On leaving **Belvedere Station (1)**, proceed south along Station Road to Lower Road; note **The Belvedere (3)** pub opposite. From here the gasholders of **Belvedere Gas Works (2)** can be seen to the north. Proceed to the left of The Belvedere as far as **13/15 Lower Park Road (4)**, the main frontages of these houses, then return to The Belvedere and turn left up Picardy Road to see the other frontages at 6/10 Picardy Road.

Continue up Picardy Road, passing **Belvedere Methodist Church (5)**, to the junction with **Halt Robin Road**, then turn left to **nos 5/8 (6)**. Return to the junction and cross to Upper Abbey Road, bearing left into **Abbey Crescent (7)**. Walk up the steps on the left to **Milton Road (7)**, then return past the terraces to the **Prince Alfred (7A)** on the corner. Turn left along Upper Abbey Road to the **Old Leather Bottle (8)**.

Rurn right down St Augustines Road to the **Church of St Augustine (9)**; try to see the interior. Turn right along Gilbert Road and Picardy Street, then left along Station Road back to the Station.

WALK No 1 (covering Frank's Park, Nuxley Road, Upper Belvedere). Distance approx five kilometres.

NB. Try to make an advance arrangement - see the gazetteer - to see the interior of All Saints Church. Bear in mind that a steep climb in Frank's Park is involved.

SECTION 'A'. On leaving **Belvedere Station (1)**, proceed south along Station Road to Lower Road, and up Lower Park Road to the left of **The Belvedere (3)** pub opposite.

SECTION 'B'. Turn left along Halt Robin Road, and bear right along the first footpath leading into **Frank's Park (10)**. You will emerge into the flat grassed area with a childrens playground in the centre of the Park. Cross over this area and take the short but quite steep path on the opposite side leading up to Tower Road and the buildings of **Bexley College (13)**.

Continue along Tower Road to Erith Road and turn right. Note the lodge at the entrance to **Trinity School (14)**, then cross the road to the **Erith Road Campus (16)**. Continue along Erith Road, noting **Redcliffe Campus, nos 37/45 (17)**, and **The Laurels (18)**.

You then reach **All Saints Church (19)**; try to see the interior. Turn left down **Nuxley Road (20)**, passing **The Vicarage** and other locations in Nuxley Road and making short detours into the side streets of **Bedwell Road, Cheshunt Road** and **Stapley Road**, until you reach the **Free Grace Baptist Chapel (20D)** on the left (ask at no 83 for permission to see the interior). Retrace steps and bear left along Albert Road until you reach **The Prince of Wales**. Look at **33/45 Woolwich Road** and **Belvedere Green (23)**.

Cross the road to **50/64 Woolwich Road (24)** and **Gloucester Road**, and **The Eardley Arms (25)**. Cross the road junction and continue along Woolwich Road until you reach **The Priory (26)**, at the corner of Picardy Road. Turn left down **Picardy Road**, noting **nos 163/167 (26)** and the **Congregational Church (28)**. Continue down Picardy Road to the bottom at The Belvedere, and cross to Station Road and Belvedere Station.

ABBEY WOOD

Introduction

The major part of Abbey Wood is a continuous belt of magnificent woodland, comprising Lesnes Abbey Woods in the east, and Bostall Heath and Bostall Woods in the west, separated by the old roads of Knee Hill and Brampton Road, which from 1888 until 1965 had been the boundary between London and Kent.

In a beautiful setting to the north of the Abbey Woods are the ancient ruins of Lesnes Abbey.

Bostall was an old settlement whose site is now covered by the Bostall Estate. It has given its name not only to the Heath, the Woods and the Estate, but also to a distinct residential area to the south of the Abbey Woods which was intensively developed in the 1930s.

Early history

The history of Abbey Wood begins with the foundation of the Augustinian Abbey of Lesnes in 1178. The buildings were largely destroyed soon after 1525 - it was dissolved by Cardinal Wolsey before the Reformation, because of its small size.

The abbey and its woodlands remained in private ownership until 1930, when they were acquired by the London County Council. The rest of the area remained farmland, very sparsely inhabited, right up to the end of the 19th century. The arrival of the railway, as early as 1849, had little impact.

Growth of housing

The first large housing development in the area was the Bostall Estate, built by the Royal Arsenal Co-operative Society between 1900 and 1914, and considered a model estate at the time.

West Heath, a stretch of heathland to the south of the Abbey Woods, was enclosed in 1815; development did not start until 1882, and even then was on a relatively small scale. But from 1930 West Heath and the area further south, which came to be called Bostall, was covered by new housing estates.

The London County Council built the Abbey Wood Estate to the north of the railway line in the 1950s, and in 1967 commenced building the large new town of Thamesmead, which adjoins and almost surrounds the Abbey Wood Estate to the north and east.

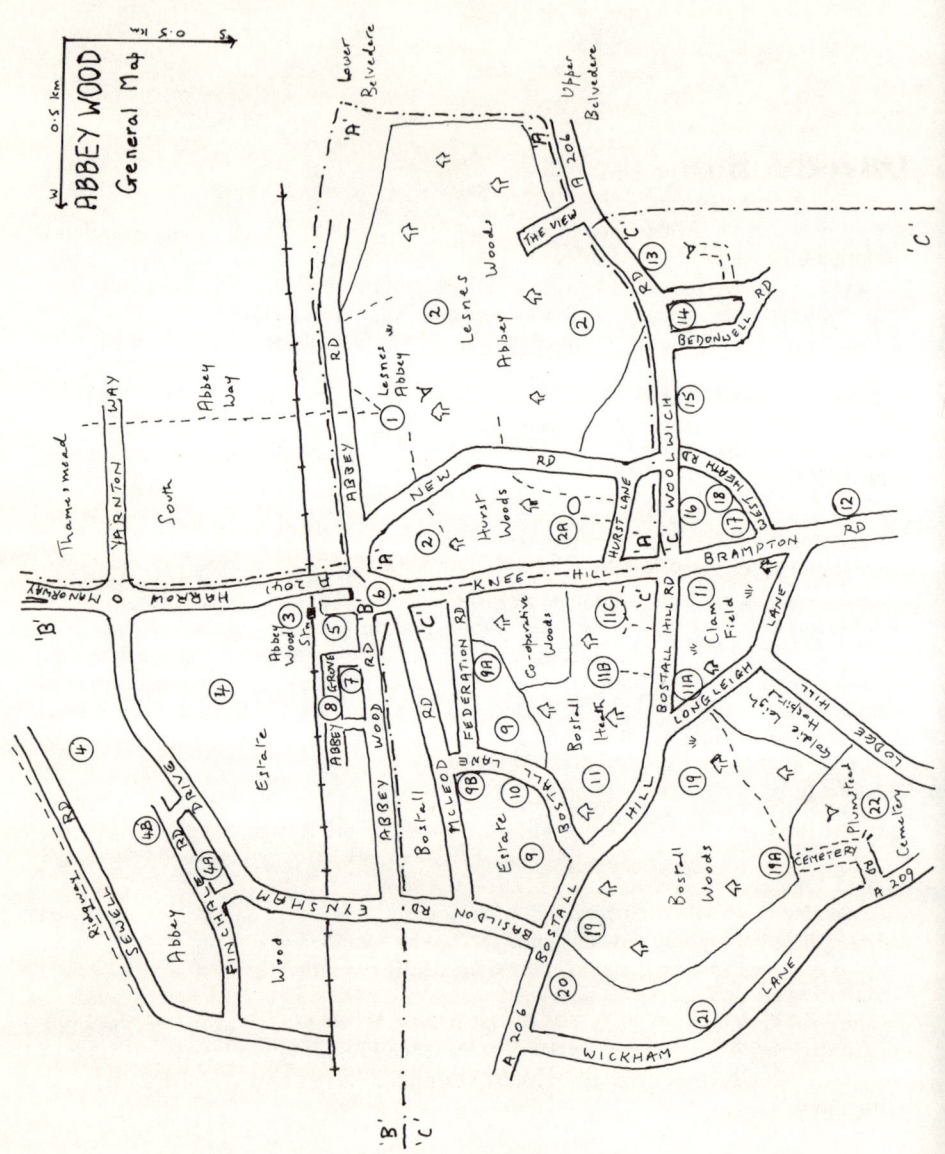

ABBEY WOOD

Gazetteer

Section 'A' LESNES ABBEY & WOODS

1. ****Lesnes Abbey,** the ruins of a 12th century Augustinian abbey, beautifully situated on a sloping site with Lesnes Abbey Woods looming to the south. The ruins basically date from 1178 to 1200, though in the 14th century the Lady Chapel was added and the west wall of the cloister rebuilt. They are the only substantial medieval abbey remains in the southern London suburbs.

The Abbey of St Mary & St Thomas the Martyr was founded in 1178 for the Augustinian or black canons by Richard de Lucy, Chief Justiciar and royal deputy to Henry II, probably as an act of penance for his role in the murder of Thomas a Becket. He died the following year, and was buried in the Chapter House.

In its day the Abbey controlled the woods to the south, and the marshlands to the north up to the Thames; they maintained the river walls and drained the marshes. It was one of the first monasteries to be dissolved - by Cardinal Wolsey in 1525, before the Reformation, because of its small size; the buildings were then largely destroyed, leaving only the Abbot's house (which remained until 1845). In 1633 the site came into the ownership of Christs Hospital, and was used mainly for farming; it remained so until acquired by the London County Council in 1930.

The site was excavated by Sir Alfred Clapham first in 1909, and again in 1939. (Finds from the excavations are in the Greenwich Borough Museum at Plumstead and in Erith Museum, at Hall Place Bexley and St Johns Church Erith; a headless effigy of a knight of the de Lucy family and a famous early 13th century illuminated missal are in the Victoria & Albert Museum.) The infirmary, to the east of the ruins, and the Abbot's house, to the north of the ruins, have not been excavated.

In 1951 the ruins were restored and excavated further by F. C. Elliston-Erwood (commemorated by a plaque set into the footings of a nave pillar by the Woolwich & District Antiquarian Society), and the footings of the buildings reconstructed in many places, so one can readily comprehend the layout of the central monastic buildings and the abbey church.

Access is best either from New Road or from Abbey Road (ascend the stairs to the bridge across the road, which is part of the Abbey Way footpath from Thamesmead South). Car parking is normally easier in Abbey Road. The site is now part of a public park, and public access is free at all times. To the west of the ruins is an Information Centre, normally open during the daytime, and the rangers office (for consultation and advice). Leaflets on the ruins and the woods are normally available at the Information Centre. Many features of the ruins are labelled.

From the Information Centre proceed directly to the west door of the Abbey Church and walk along the nave; note the bases of shafts along the north aisle, and at the end a grave slab. Walk up the steps into the choir (which was the tower crossing); note the substantial bases and shafts of the western piers. There are some original tiles where the south aisle leads into the south transept. From the choir continue straight ahead into the presbytery, and up the steps to the High Altar. Note on the right the Lady Chapel of 1371, which has an unusual tiled sunken chamber (used for storing holy relics etc).

Return to the crossing and walk down the steps, turn right and right again into the north transept. Note the three chapels, each with bases of shafts and a grave slab; beyond is the sacristy. From the north transept walk down the steps into the east walk of the cloister; note on the left some original tiles leading to the north aisle. Turn right, passing the book locker and a long stone bench which retains some original tiles, to the entrance to the Chapter House, which has reconstructed wall seating.

Continue along the east walk of the cloister and you immediately come to the slype (or passage), leading to the infirmary doorway. Beyond was the Infirmary, which has not been excavated; however, the footings to the left may have been connected with the Infirmary. Return to the cloister, and to the right are stairs leading up to the dorter (or dormitory). Walk down the steps to the undercroft of the dorter; note the two round headed windows in the taller west wall. Beyond the room at the end of the dorter is the reredorter (or latrines), with two deep pits.

Return to the cloister outside the dorter, going through a modern Gothic doorway. Turn right along the north walk, which is alongside the ruins of the refectory. The high north wall of the refectory has clear remains of a staircase, lit by two tiny lancet windows, which led to the refectory pulpit. At the end of the refectory note the mulberry tree outside, which was near the site of the Abbot's House (which has not been excavated); and in the north-west corner, a serving hatch from the kitchen, which was outside the cloister. The original kitchen, however, was the room to the west of the refectory; beyond it was the outer parlour, and to its south an outer room was the brewhouse.

Turn along the west walk of the cloister; at the end turn right through the 14th century doorway, which is well-preserved. Note along the north wall of the nave some holes which were used for wooden supports for the pentise, or covered walkway, which led to the western processional door. Go through this doorway and back to the west door of the church.

On a terrace beyond the flower beds to the south is the Well (now covered), from which water was conveyed to the site by leaden pipes; the well was fed by a pool in the south of the woods which has now dried up. Depressions on either side of the site were used by the Abbey as a fish-pond (to the west) and a dew-pond (to the east).

A good view of the ruins can be obtained by ascending the steps into the woods behind the High Altar.

2. **Lesnes Abbey Woods.** An extensive area of rolling woodland, interrupted by deep valleys, some with extremely steep slopes. The overall effect is extremely picturesque. The woods were acquired by the London County Council at the same time as the abbey ruins in 1930, and are largely classified as ancient woodland. The woods also incorporate **Hurst Woods**, between New Road and Knee Hill.

There is a wide variety of trees, the dominant large trees being the sweet chestnut and the oak. There are also large groups of birch, ash, hornbeam, wild cherry, hawthorn, maple, hazel, and several wild service trees.

Although the woods are dense and precipitous in places, there is a good network of well-surfaced paths. A self-guided trail to the woodlands of just over three kilometres may be obtained at the Information Centre near the Abbey ruins, and first time visitors are strongly recommended to follow this trail. Bear in mind that it includes some quite steep ascents and descents.
The main places of interest, all included in the trail, are as follows:

(i) Three large fenced enclosures, immediately south of the abbey ruins, which protect the famous spring displays of wild daffodils, bluebells and wood anemones. In the middle enclosure is a separate fenced area containing some rich **fossil beds**; the fossils most commonly found are shells and sharks teeth, which may date back 56 million years, when the climate was tropical and the London area was covered by a warm shallow lagoon. *Authorisation to enter may be obtained at the ranger's office.*

(ii) A chalk pit, deep and dramatic, where chalk was excavated before 1930 for use on the farmland around the Abbey site.

(iii) In Hurst Woods, a beautiful ornamental pool, called **Pine Pond (2A)**. It was created in the late 19th century as part of the grounds of Hurst House, which was located to the south of Hurst Lane. The pond can also be readily accessed by footpaths leading from Hurst Lane.

It is also worth entering the woods from the south, at the end of The View, off Woolwich Road. The main path on the right leads after a short distance to an attractive area of heathland. The path on the left leads quickly to a ridge, with steep and delightful ravines on both sides; 'giant steps' lead down to the further ravine.

ABBEY WOOD

Gazetteer

Section 'B' LOWER ABBEY WOOD
(See map on page 68)

3. Abbey Wood Station. A modern station with a striking design, its roof swooping up to an acutely angled point at the entrance. It was built in 1975 to replace an earlier building, and at the same time a level crossing was replaced by the bridge. The station was originally opened in 1849.

4. Abbey Wood Estate. A large estate, built by the London County Council between 1956 and 1959. There is a strong feeling of isolation - it is cut off to the north by the Southern Outfall Sewer, to the west by allotments, and to the south by the railway; to the east it is separated from Thamesmead South by Harrow Manorway. The only road access is by Eynsham Drive, which enters from the south on a flyover over the railway, and by Harrow Manorway. *(For the Southern Outfall Sewer and Ridgway, see Belvedere 34.)*

In Eynsham Drive is the centre, with a small shopping parade, library and **William Temple Church (4A)**, a modern church of 1966 with a thin spire and bright stained glass in the interior *(contact: 5 Finchale Road, 0181-310 5614)*.

To the north, in Finchale Road, is **St Davids Church (4B)**, a Roman Catholic church of 1964 with a colourful figure of St David on the entrance wall; the interior *(contact: 138 Godstow Road, 0181-311 2727)* has bright stained glass.

5. The Abbey Arms, Wilton Road. A pub, basically c1860, but considerably altered when rebuilt after a fire in 1900.

6. The Harrow Inn. An impressive pub with deep eaves, of 1860.

7. Church of St Michael & All Angels, Abbey Wood Road. A bulky but rather grand red brick church, by the firm of Sir Arthur Blomfield & Son 1908. The interior *(contact: Vicarage, Conference Road, 0181-311 0377)* is spacious and very Gothic.

8. Church of St Benet, Abbey Grove. An impressive Roman Catholic church of 1909, with a great romanesque-arched doorway and a triplet of windows above separated by bulbous Saxon pillars. Unremarkable interior, altered in the 1960s. The presbytery *(contact 0181-211 2594)* next door at no 31 is in similar style and forms an integral part of the building.

ABBEY WOOD

Gazetteer

Section 'C' BOSTALL
(See map on page 68)

9. Bostall Estate. This estate under the shadow of Bostall Heath was built by the Royal Arsenal Co-operative Society between 1900 and 1914. It is bounded by Bostall Heath, Basildon Road, Abbey Wood Road and Knee Hill, with McLeod Road the main road running through. The estate consists of long terraces in varied styles, and many houses have ornamental flourishes and distinctive brick patterns. There has been considerable extension and infill since the last war, particularly in the western part, but the area retains a distinct Edwardian atmosphere. The estate is now mostly owned by a housing association.

The **Federation Day Centre (9A)**, Federation Road, formerly the Federation Hall, was the works dining hall during construction of the estate. In the south-west corner of the grounds is the sealed top of a chalk mine, with a grill to allow passage to a colony of bats. The mine is 20 metres below ground, and was used during the construction of the estate; it was finally sealed c1960. *Ask permission from the Manager before looking around, or ring 0181-311 8519 in advance.*

The Co-op supermarket in McLeod Road has on the side facing Bostall Lane a splendid ornamental **plaque (9B)** of 1900 commemorating the commencement of the building of the Estate. There is also a smaller tablet commemorating the opening of the first Co-op shop there in 1912.

> Two large farms to the north of Bostall Heath, Bostall Farm and the adjoining Sussex Place, were acquired by the then Royal Arsenal Co-operative Society in 1886 and in 1899 respectively. In 1900 it was decided to convert the land to a housing estate. Building started in 1900, and continued to 1909; it resumed in 1912 but stopped in 1914 after 1052 houses had been built. The Caravan Club site, in the beautiful parkland setting of Co-operative Woods on Federation Road, was the works site during construction of the estate. The RACS was founded in Woolwich in 1868, and absorbed by the Co-operative Wholesale Society in 1985. Many road names in the area have Co-op associations.

10. Alexander McLeod School, originally known as Bostall Lane School, situated on the corner of Bostall Lane and Fuchsia Street. An impressive though rather heavy London School Board building of 1903, relieved by the balustrades and urns on top of the central section (best seen from the rear). Alexander McLeod was a founder and the first full-time secretary of the RACS.

11. *Bostall Heath consists of heathland with gorse and broom at the top of Bostall Hill, and dense woods and deep ravines on the steep slopes to the north. The heath

74 - ABBEY WOOD

stretches across Bostall Hill to include **Clam Field**, a grassed open space fringed by belts of trees.

<blockquote>Bostall Heath was acquired for the people by the Metropolitan Board of Works in 1877. As in the case of Plumstead Common and Shoulder of Mutton Green, Welling, which were acquired at the same time, this followed attempts by Queens College Oxford, which owned all these lands, to deny public access. Clam Field was acquired by the London County Council in 1894.</blockquote>

The old **Heathkeeper's Lodge (11A)** at the corner of Bostall Hill and Longleigh Lane, a rather fanciful building with tiled upper floor, was built 1880 by the Metropolitan Board of Works. On the other side of Longleigh Lane is a horse trough, late 19th century.

In the south-east three buildings occupy enclaves on the Heath: **Greenwich & Bexley Cottage Hospice (11B)**, a handsome building of 1994 with great sloping roofs and tiled gables, on the site of Shornells, a house of 1873 which became a training centre and guest-house for the RACS. and was destroyed by fire 1989; **Bostall House**, modern, on the site of a mid 19th century house; and **The Belvedere Private Clinic (11C)**, formerly called **The Cottage**, a large and rather eccentric mid 19th century building, much altered, with fine bay windows, bargeboarding and other decorative features.

12. Church of St Andrew, Brampton Road. The parish church of Bostall Heath. An attractive church of 1957, with the roofs swooping down on both sides. Striking interior *(contact the Vicarage next door, 0181 303 9332)*, with wooden ribs stretching to the apex, making it look like an upturned boat. Note the fine mid 19th century chamber organ. The church is linked to a hall of 1972.

13. 115 Woolwich Road, formerly known as **Westheath House**, a magnificent house in classical style of 1872. Sir Tom Callender of BICC, who lived here c1900-21, made extensions in 1913; the building alongside the road was converted from the stables, and there have been other alterations. It is set back from the road; go round the back into Milford Close for a view (over the garages) of the rear, with its pairs of Doric columns.

14. 137 Woolwich Road is a startling white concrete cubist house, by D. R. Surti 1965. The ground floor supports four projecting blocks, which are the bedrooms, notable for the juxtaposition of vertical and horizontal windows.

15. Lessness Park. All that remains of the grounds of this mid 19th century mansion (demolished in 1933) is a narrow green with a splendid line of trees along Woolwich Road.

16. St Josephs Campus, an annexe of Bexley College, is an interesting complex which appears like one long mid 19th century Italianate building, but which is in fact a late 19th century building whose frontage was quadrupled in length by a series of extensions from 1913 to c1935.

Its building history is intriguing. The earliest part is the middle section (bearing the inscription 1904-1954) with four bay windows, probably of the 1880s; it was acquired by the Congregation of the Daughters of Jesus as a convent in 1904, and became St Josephs Convent School in 1905. It was extended to the west in 1913 by a rather elegant section with a balcony, and this became the chapel. In 1925 there was a further extension to the west forming an end pavilion with a portico. A pair of houses of 1902 to the east was acquired c1930, and c1935 was linked to the original building by a section with two end porches. A large modern extension was erected behind in 1956. The school closed in 1979, and the site became part of Bexley College.

So looking at the building from left to right are: the Edwardian brick houses of 1902; a section flanked by two porches c1935; the original late 19th century building with four bay windows; a section of 1913 with a balcony; and at the end a projecting pavilion of 1925.

17. 46/48 West Heath Road, an impressive pair, probably of the 1880s, with doorways flanked by Corinthian columns.

18. 32 West Heath Road, a striking house, probably c1900, with its central entrance recessed between two full-height bays, one gabled and one castellated.

19. *Bostall Woods. A picturesque area of woodland, dense in places but interspersed with forest glades, on the slopes of Bostall Hill. There is a wide variety of trees, the dominant large trees being the oak, sweet chestnut and birch.

The woods were formerly known as Old Park Wood, and included the grounds of Old Park House and Goldie Leigh Lodge, both early 19th century mansions. The woods were purchased by the London County Council in 1892 and were renamed Bostall Woods, and the houses were eventually demolished.

Part of the woods was used from 1902 as Goldie Leigh Hospital, a large complex set up as homes for children in care, which became a hostel for handicapped children; this use continued until 1988, and the future of the site is now uncertain.

The site of Old Park House is now a glade located between the Green Chain Walk and the path along the boundary of Goldie Leigh Hospital; it is best approached by following the Walk signpost from Longleigh Lane.

Woodside Cottage (19A), the house c1902 at the end of Cemetery Road, was a lodge alongside a driveway to Goldie Leigh Hospital; the old driveway, flanked by tall lime trees, can be reached by taking the footpath beyond the lodge and parallel to its garden for about 100 yards, then descending some steps to the right.

Under the eastern edge of the woods is a network of chalk mines, which were in use until the mid 19th century.

20. Maybloom Club, Bostall Hill. A grand classical building, built as Plumstead Workingmens Club c1912, which became the Maybloom Club, another workingmens club, in 1926. It has a fine frontispiece with balustrade and pediment, and rows of round-headed windows on either side.

21. St Pauls School, Wickham Lane, formerly Oakmere School. A large and splendid building, with tower, cupola and many ornate features, front and rear. It was built by the London School Board c1903, primarily for children at Goldie Leigh Hospital. Modern extension to the north.

22. Plumstead Cemetery, Cemetery Road. This cemetery of 1890 occupies a spectacular hillside site, with magnificent views, particularly of the adjoining Bostall Woods. The arched gateway is echoed by the porte-cochere between the chapels. The larger chapel c1898 is in an ornate Gothic style with a tall spire. Nearby is a pink obelisk to men who were killed in explosions at the Royal Arsenal in 1903.

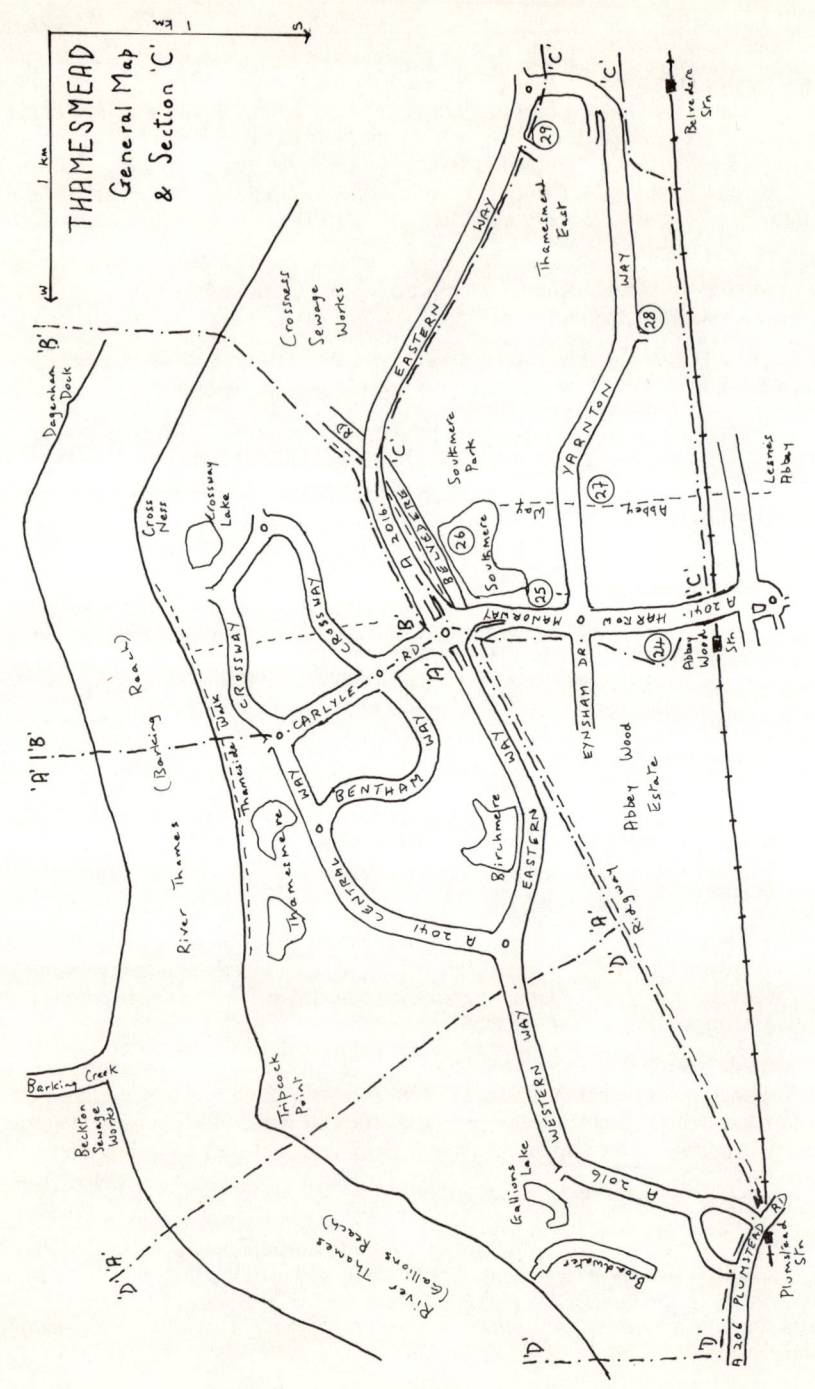

THAMESMEAD

Introduction

Thamesmead is a 'new town', still in the course of construction, on land reclaimed from the Plumstead and Erith marshes, most of which formed part of the Royal Arsenal. It was planned by the Greater London Council and construction started in 1967. Since 1987, after the GLC had been abolished, it has been owned and managed by Thamesmead Town, which is a private company. Now the housing is being built mainly by private developers, but also by housing associations. It is expected to be completed by c2010, with a final population of about 40,000 persons.

Its distinctive landscape and waterscape give Thamesmead a very positive identity, and make it unique in the London area. Unlike the Docklands developments on the opposite side of the river, parkland and waterland are integrated with the housing sections and shopping centres within a thoughtfully planned environment, and there is a network of footpaths throughout the developed area.

Nevertheless, Thamesmead has very much the atmosphere of a town apart, as its boundaries with neighbouring parts of London are so emphatic - the Thames to the north, the Royal Arsenal to the west, the Crossness Sewage Works and the industrial zone of Belvedere to the east, the Southern Outfall Sewer and the railway line to the south.

The Augustinian monks
In the 12th century part of the land was under the control of the Augustinian Abbey of Lesnes, and there is evidence that the monks tried hard to drain the marshes and reclaim the land. The ruins of the Abbey remain on higher ground to the south *(see Abbey Wood 1)*, and a vantage point by the woods beyond the ruins provides a wide view over Thamesmead.

London's Sewage
In 1862 the Southern Outfall Sewer was constructed within a raised embankment through the area as part of Sir Joseph Bazalgette's comprehensive sewage system for London, and the embankment remains a dominant feature of the landscape. The sewer itself ends in the Crossness Sewage Treatment Works. This is now a modern establishment of 1964, but the old beam engine house of 1865 still survives *(see Belvedere 34A)*, and is in the course of restoration.

The Arsenal, and the tumps
In the late 19th century the Royal Arsenal in Woolwich expanded eastwards to acquire much of the land which is now Thamesmead, but from 1918 onwards the use

of this vast area began to decline and eventually in 1965 the GLC purchased the land from the Government.

The most important physical features remaining from the Arsenal days are the nine moated magazines or 'tumps' of c1890. Five tumps have been integrated into the 'new town' as ecology or amenity areas, whilst the other four are not at present readily accessible to the public. Many of the tumps still retain the old brick walls which were built to protect them and limit the effect of explosions. Other survivals include part of the Arsenal canal of 1812-16, and stretches of 19th century brick wall.

Flood defence and drainage

At high tide the land is below the water level of the river. From 1965, as part of the flood defence programme which included the Thames Barrier at Charlton, the GLC raised the river bank throughout the area. The high level path of the Thameside Walk now runs along part of the raised bank for over a kilometre. In due course the Walk will be extended along the entire five kilometres of river frontage.

The old problem of marsh drainage has been solved by creating a network of lakes and canals whose level is controlled by a main Pumping Station at Thamesmere. Each residential zone has its own lake, as does the town centre, and the canals have become an attractive feature in many housing areas, particularly in Thamesmead North.

Housing styles

The early stages of housing development were in the style of the 1960s, with high rise point blocks and long spine blocks in concrete, overwhelming, heavy and rather dramatic. The original plan was for this style to dominate throughout, but in practice the style was only used in Thamesmead South and on the eastern edges of Thamesmead Central.

In the 1970s architectural fashion began to change, and later developments were small scale in concept and vernacular in style, with intimate and irregular village-like groupings of houses in closes, use of red tiled roofs and coloured bricks, etc. However, some of the more recent schemes show a return to a more urban concept.

Undeveloped areas

Large areas are still undeveloped, and are not accessible to the public. However, 'Thamesmead Urban Safaris' are often organised as part of the Greenwich Festival in June, and these include visits to locations of interest in the undeveloped areas.

The most interesting such location is The Twin Tumps - two large tumps located at the south end of the Thamesmere Extension *(see 4)*. Though surrounded by moats, these tumps have an inter-connecting series of causeways. In the centre of each tump are grassed meadows, and all around are birch groves. The whole area has a special atmosphere.

Other such locations are: an old powder house, probably late 19th century, covered in creepers and undergrowth, to the west of the Thamesmere Extension; an old proof-butt, probably late 19th century, also covered by creepers and undergrowth, at the northern end of the Eastgate wall *(see 34)*; the remains of two jetties used by the Arsenal (originally of 1872, reconstructed 1922), on the river wall near Broadwater.

The mound visible from Merbury Road in Thamesmead West was created by the GLC during excavation.

The Zones

Thamesmead is officially divided into six zones, of which four are mainly residential - Thamesmead Central, Thamesmead North, Thamesmead South and Thamesmead West; and two largely industrial - Thamesmead East and Thamesmead South-West. In Thamesmead South-West are the West Thamesmead Business Park and, though strictly not part of Thamesmead, Belmarsh Prison and the Crown Court. Thamesmead Central, North and West are the areas which once formed part of the Royal Arsenal.

Thamesmead Central

This zone is at present largely residential, but it includes the first phase of the town centre, completed in 1986, and a large undeveloped area. The residential part was developed from 1971 and was largely completed by 1980; however, some estates to the west of Birchmere have yet to be commenced. Other residential areas are planned for the future around Thamesmere and the town centre.

The town centre is at present quite small, but an expansion to include more retail and leisure facilities is planned for the future. There is another local shopping centre, The Moorings. There are three lakes, Thamesmere, Birchmere and the Thamesmere Extension, as well as canals and tumps.

Thamesmead North

This zone is almost entirely residential. It was developed from 1977, and a large part has now been built, though several schemes have yet to be commenced in the east of the zone. Its lake, Crossway Lake, with its two islands, is most attractive but access is limited as developments in the area around are not yet completed. There is a small local shopping centre at Manor Close. This section has the most interesting housing schemes, and the canals and tumps have been most successfully integrated here.

Thamesmead South

This zone consists mainly of the almost entirely residential zone of Thamesmead South. It was the first to be developed, from 1967, and was completed by 1982. It incorporates the largest lake, Southmere. It has two local shopping centres, Tavy Bridge and Greenmead.

It is isolated from other parts of Thamesmead by the parallel barriers to the north of the Southern Outfall Sewer and the Spine Road (A2016). To the west it merges into the Abbey Wood Estate *(see Abbey Wood 4)*, and the main offices of Thamesmead Town are situated on the edge of the area at this point. The only access to the Crossness Sewage Works *(see Belvedere 34)* is through this zone.

Thamesmead West

This zone is at present largely residential, developed from 1979. Some districts have now been completed, but many schemes are yet to be built along the riverside and to the north. It has a local shopping centre, Broadwaters, and a lake, Gallions Lake. It incorporates the old Arsenal canal, now known as Broadwater.

At present its links are closer with Plumstead than with other zones of Thamesmead; it is separated by a large undeveloped area from Thamesmead Central, over a kilometre away.

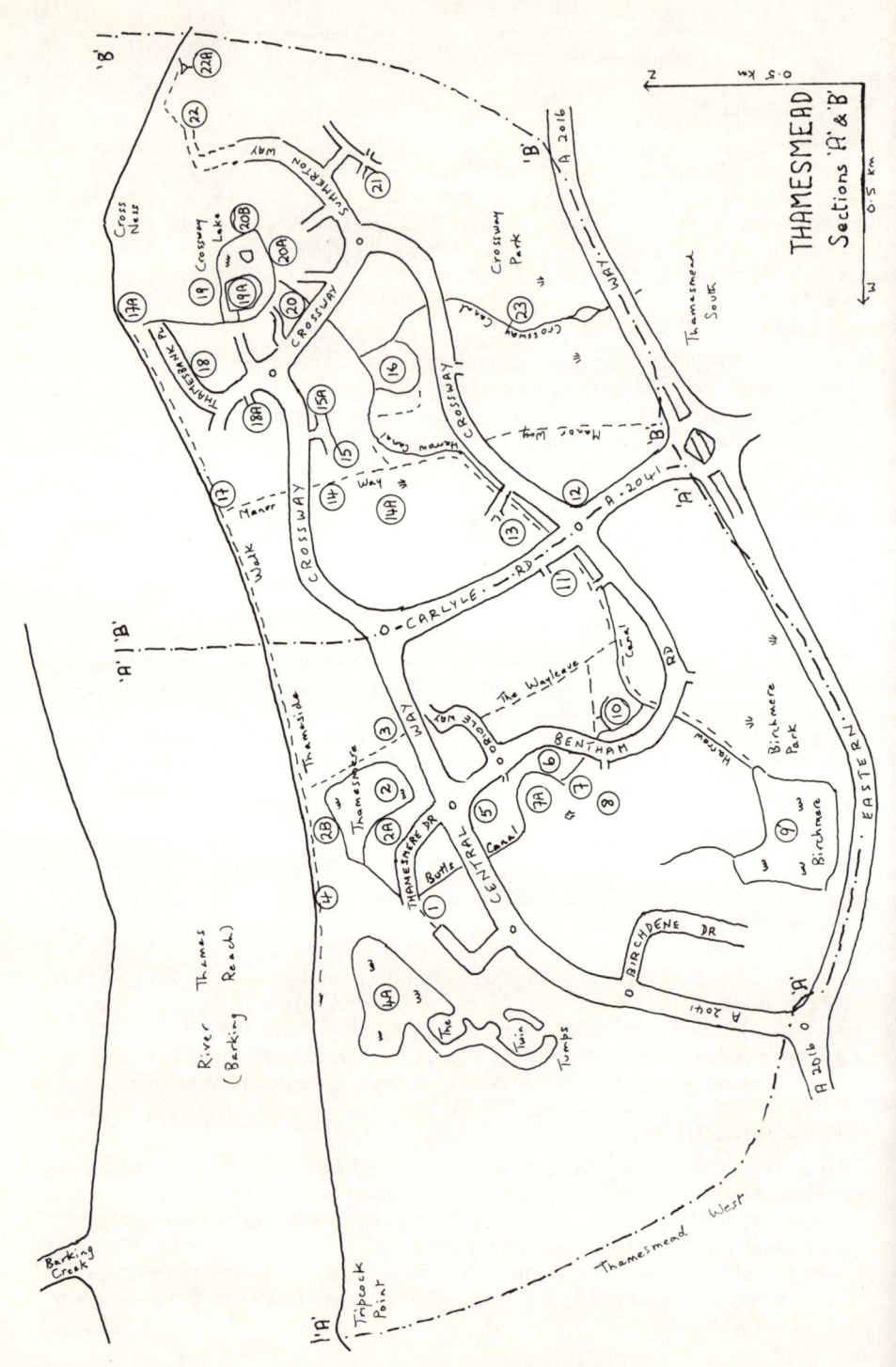

THAMESMEAD

Gazetteer

SECTION 'A' THAMESMEAD CENTRAL

1. **Shopping Centre.** The centre, completed 1986, is at present quite small, and takes the form of a square, with one side occupied by an open air market (on Fridays and Saturdays). The Butts Canal runs right through the centre, with paved walks alongside. There are two foot-bridges over the canal, both with red pantiled roofs producing a pagoda-like impression. The retail buildings (which incorporate an attractive pub, The Wat Tyler) are in vernacular cottage-style, with canopied walkways and pantiled verandahs, and there is positive use of blue and red.

The central feature of the square is a tall **clock tower** which is a prominent landmark; the clock and belfry are of 1762, from the Great Storehouse of the Royal Naval Dockyard at Deptford, and in 1987 were placed on top of a severely classical modern tower. Opposite the tower, on the other side of the canal, is a fountain flanked by two British cannon of 1847 and 1853.

On either side of the shopping centre is an example of the K6 type of **red cast-iron telephone kiosks**, imported into the area. The K6 type was designed by Sir Giles Gilbert Scott in 1935, and incorporates rectangular panes of glass, whereas the K2 type, designed by Scott in 1927, has all panes of glass of the same size.

2. **Thamesmere.** A large lake, with two prominent buildings on its banks - the **Thamesmere Leisure Centre (2A)**, a handsome building of 1986 in dark brick, incorporating a swimming-pool; and the ***Pumping Station (2B)**, c1976, with its spectacular group of four giant Archimedean screws (which remove excess water from the lake and canal network). The screws can be seen best from a terrace within the Leisure Centre, but access to the lakeside itself at this point is not normally open to the public; however, there are good views over the lake from several points around.

3. **Linton Mead School**, Central Way. An attractive dark low-lying building of 1986, with a striking shallow roof of black slate crowned by a small glazed pyramid. The view from the road is obstructed, and it is best viewed from the footpath to the west which leads to the Thameside Walk.

4. *Thameside Walk (west part). This is part of the Thameside Walk which at present extends for over a kilometre between Tripcock Point in the west and Cross Ness in the east, though it does not yet reach either of these headlands. There are two parallel walkways the whole length - the low level path, alongside the river; and the high level path, on a raised bank which is part of the river flood defences. Both paths are wide and well landscaped, with special viewpoints and seating areas.

Access to the west part of the Walk is by a public footpath which starts just west of Linton Mead School and runs alongside the private road to the Thamesmere Pumping Station. On reaching the high level path, turn left.

There are excellent wide views along Barking Reach. On the opposite side of the river are, to the left, Barking Creek Barrier, with its blue falling radial gate, by Binnie & Partners c1982; and alongside, Beckton Sewage Works, with the outfall clearly visible.

On the landward side the views are interesting. You pass to the rear of the Thamesmere Pumping Station *(see 2B)*, with its dramatic warning in large letters for Thames shipping - 'Warning - Thames Barrier Control Zone - obtain permission to proceed beyond this point. When amber light is flashing, navigate with extreme caution. When red light is flashing, STOP, all navigation prohibited.' Across the lake Thamesmere *(see 2)* can be seen the Town Centre and its clock tower *(see 1)*, and Thamesmere Leisure Centre *(see 2A)*.

Proceeding further you come to an undeveloped area, with the only view at present of a large lake, the **Thamesmere Extension (4A)**, which will eventually be linked to Thamesmere.

Retrace steps to the access footpath. From this point the Walk passes through a lengthy central section, totally undeveloped, before reaching the east part of the Walk. *For a description of the east part, see 17.*

5. Gallions Reach Health Centre. A pleasant building by Derek Stow of 1986, basically in vernacular style but with high-tech features and striking use of red.

Behind the car park is a section of high brick wall remaining from an old Arsenal firing range *(see also 8)*.

6. St Pauls Ecumenical Church Centre, Bentham Road. A modern building of 1978, containing two churches, Roman Catholic (to the right of the corridor) and Anglican / Free Church (to the left).

It is worth viewing the interior *(contact: 0181-310 6814)*. The church to the left has two striking paintings, The Madonna and Child (against a Thamesmead background) and The Last Supper, both by Graeme Willson 1983. The former painting was originally in the other church.

7. Butts Wood. A delightful small area of birch woodland, fringed by Butts Canal. To the north is **Tump 54 (7A)** *(see introduction, page 78)*, surrounded by a brick wall, and a moat now forming part of the canal. To the west is a high ridge, with fine views on all sides.

8. Waterfield School. An extensive one-storey building of 1977 in a high-tech style, with much use of vivid red and yellow.

By the east entrance, off Waterfield Close, is a section of high brick wall remaining from an old Arsenal firing range *(see also 5)*.

9. Birchmere. There is general public access to this large lake, except on the western side, where a housing scheme, Pitfield Crescent, consisting largely of houses with classical porticos, was constructed c1989. The large grassed expanse of Birchmere Park adjoins to the east. There is a good view from the north bank of Shooters Hill and of Bostall Woods and Lesnes Abbey Woods in the distance.

10. *Tump 53 Ecology Park *(see introduction, page 78)*. This tump is preserved as a nature study area; it is at present the only wildlife area in Thamesmead to which there is ready public access. The tump is now a small meadow surrounded by high earth banks and a brick wall, and encircled by a lengthy section of moat, which merges into a large area of reedbeds. The moat is raised above the level of the Butts Canal by means of weirs.

It is accessible from a footpath running between Bentham Road and The Wayleave, which leads to a causeway through the moat and into the tump.

11. The Moorings Centre. A local shopping centre of 1976 with a pedestrian terrace overlooking the Harrow Canal. The centre incorporates a pub, Wildfowler Inn; note the tiled mural by Kenneth & Ann Clark 1978 on the side wall. Its canal-side site and the use of dark red and purple brick make this centre quite attractive.

THAMESMEAD

Gazetteer

SECTION 'B' THAMESMEAD NORTH
(See map on page 80)

12. Thamesmead Boiler House. Built c1970, it supplies heating and hot water to large parts of Thamesmead, and is one of the largest community heating systems in the country. It is a striking building with its six tall boiler chimneys.

13. Moorings Reach. This housing development of 1994 has long terraces with a steep central gable. During excavations for Slocum Close in the development, a wooden platform from the New Stone Age (c3000 BC) was discovered.

14. Manor Way. This footpath leads for about a kilometre from the Thameside Walk down to the Spine Road. The most attractive section is roughly midway where it runs alongside Harrow Canal.

To the west is **Manorway Green (14A)**, an attractive small park which incorporates the mound of **Tump 47** *(see introduction, page 78)* with its hollow converted into an amphitheatre; the area all around here is rural and most attractive.

15. Manor Close. This housing section, completed 1990, has a rather formal pattern, but there is an attractive sense of enclosure. It incorporates a small local centre, and a community centre, a temple-like building which closes the view from the south. Note the repetitive pattern of projecting white piers in the houses and the community centre. It terminates in a crescent around a green, in a pleasant rural setting around Harrow Canal.

Opposite Manor Close within the semi-circle of Grange Crescent is **Tump 48 (15A)** *(see introduction, page 78)*. A small green has been made from the hollow of the tump. This is perhaps the least interesting of all the tump conversions.

16. Tump 52 *(see introduction, page 78)*. This tump, surrounded by a moat and partly by its old brick wall, has been converted in quite an interesting way, with stockades enclosing children's playgrounds.

On the east side of the tump is a canal junction, a pleasant spot where the waters of Harrow Canal, Crossway Canal and the moat meet.

17. *Thameside Walk (east part). This is part of the Thameside Walk which at present extends for over a kilometre between Tripcock Point in the west and Cross Ness in the east, though it does not yet reach either of these headlands. There are two parallel walkways the whole length - the low level path, alongside the river; and the high level path, on a raised bank which is part of the river flood defences. Both paths are wide and well landscaped, with special viewpoints and seating areas.

The main access to the east part of the Walk is by the footpath Manor Way. There is also access from Thamesbank Place and The Cascade *(see below)*.
There are excellent wide views along Barking Reach. On the opposite side of the river can be seen, to the left, Barking Creek Barrier, with its blue falling radial gate, by Binnie & Partners c1982; alongside, Beckton Sewage Works; and in the distance to the right, the oil storage depot by Dagenham Dock.
From the end of Manor Way, turn right. You pass a battery of four British cannon of 1830, and the housing development, Thamesbank Place *(see 18)*. The final section of this part of the Walk ends in **The Cascade (17A)**, a sequence of steps which zigzags down to a terrace overlooking the short canal leading into Crossway Lake; note the intriguing patterns of the tubular steel used at both ends of The Cascade.
Although the Walk finishes here, if the way is not barred, you can continue eastward. You pass the beacon at the Crossness headland, and then two platforms in mid-river, one marking the outfall for Barking Reach Power Station opposite, and the other used by the National Rivers Authority; but you then come, frustratingly, to an iron fence before a good view of the old works at the Crossness Sewage Works can be obtained *(see also 22A.)*
West of Manor Way the Walk passes through a lengthy central section, totally undeveloped, before reaching the west part of the Walk. *For a description of the west part, see 4.*

18. Thamesbank Place. This development c1988 in 'Docklands vernacular' style has a strong urban quality, with its access road passing a series of compact closes and terminating in a crescent. Its location is outstanding, with the river to the north and the canal leading to Crossway Lake to the east.
On the other side of Copperfield Road is **Drake Crescent (18A)**, consisting of a large classical crescent and central block c1989, also strongly urban in character.

19. *Crossway Lake. This lake, with its masses of reeds, is highly attractive. There are two islands, the larger being **Tump 39 (19A)** - the bridge to the island at the end of Watersmeet Way is at present closed, but it is intended that the tump will in due course become a nature study area. There is a narrow footpath along the west and south sides of the lake, from The Cascade to Templar Drive, but it is difficult to follow in parts because of trees and undergrowth.

20. Lakeview. This housing section, designed by Phippen, Randal & Parkes c1987, comprising Pointer Close and Eastgate Close, conveys something of the atmosphere of an enclosed Italian village. Two of the housing terraces arch across the Crossway Canal, just before it joins Crossway Lake *(see 19)*. The bridge at the end of the canal gives a view of the lake and its islands.
Templar Drive (20A), a less dramatic development immediately to the east, by the same architects c1989, incorporates a jetty on the lake. Beyond can be seen the brick walls of the **'square tump' (20B)**, originally an Arsenal storage area of c1890.

21. Courtland Grove. In this pleasing housing development c1987, all houses have dentilled pediments over gables and doorways, and some houses have amazing wooden latticework.

22. Riverside Golf Course, opened 1993 in a wild setting at the end of Summerton Way. It has a pleasant **clubhouse**, vaguely high-tech with prominent use of green, with a verandah and balcony framed by green posts extending right round the building.

From the entrance to the Golf Club a footpath leads to the Thames. After a short distance you come to the fence of Crossness Sewage Works; here is the best **view (22A)** from outside of the Old Works. You can also see at this point two mid-river platforms, one marking the outfall for Barking Reach Power Station opposite, and the other used by the National Rivers Authority.

23. Crossway Park, a large grassed park around the Crossway Canal. Before the canal continues under Eastern Way and into Southmere, the canal is dammed by a weir to form a small lake, and the area around here is most attractive.

THAMESMEAD

Gazetteer

SECTION 'C' THAMESMEAD SOUTH
(See map on page 76)

24. The main offices of **Thamesmead Town**, Harrow Manor Way *(phone 0181-310 1500)*. The offices include an Information Centre, where an excellent map of Thamesmead can be obtained.

Flanking the entrance are two French guns of 1808 brought from Chatham Dockyard. By the car park at the rear there are a number of old guns (some Spanish, Swedish, and French), as well as anchors and mooring bollards, mostly discovered during clearance work around the old Arsenal canal in Thamesmead West; they are mainly 18th and 19th century, but there are two culverins of 1650 & 1690.

25. Tavy Bridge Centre. This was the first local shopping centre, built in 1972. It is situated on a first floor deck at the south end of the lake Southmere, and is approached by a grand staircase from Yarnton Way. Like the housing blocks of Binsey Walk (of which it is an appendage) and Coralline Walk, built in the early 1970s, it is concrete and harsh.

A wide bare concrete terrace overlooks a concrete expanse which was originally the shallow end of the lake, separated from the lake proper by a weir. A bridge slopes down from the Centre across this expanse to street level on the other side, and two buildings thrust out over it on columns - the Pyramid Club and the quite dramatic **Lakeside Health Centre**, by Derek Stow, both of 1972.

26. *Southmere. The largest and most attractive of the Thamesmead lakes, and the only lake at present to which there is full public access. In the east part of the lake is a small wooded island.

The footpath all round the lake provides a series of dramatic views. In this setting, even the concrete spine block of Binsey Walk with its jagged outline to the west, and the concrete point blocks of Hartslock Drive to the south look imposing when viewed from the opposite side of the lake. To the east is **Southmere Park**, with a high ridge affording excellent views.

27. Abbey Way. This pleasant footpath leads for about a kilometre from Southmere to the Lesnes Abbey ruins and woods *(see Abbey Wood 1, 2)*. It is mostly on a ridge, with good views, and is carried by bridges across main roads and the railway line.

28. Greenmead. This housing section, completed 1982, has a remarkably rural setting, with small greens and longer green fingers penetrating amongst the low terraces of houses and flats. The housing is all in one style, vernacular revival in dark brick, in informal and irregular groupings. The area has a pleasant local shopping centre in similar style and incorporating some intriguing metal sculpture.

29. Plant Construction plc, Hailey Road. An industrial unit in the industrial zone of Thamesmead East. It is a simple but striking hangar, covered by a skin of corrugated metal, coloured bright blue, with an end wall of dark glass. It was considered a pioneering building when originally constructed by Norman Foster Associates in 1973 for Modern Art Glass.

THAMESMEAD

Gazetteer

SECTION 'D' THAMESMEAD WEST
(See map on page 90)

30. Broadwaters Centre. This local shopping centre of 1982 is sited by the old Arsenal canal, Broadwater *(see 32)*.

31. Wren Path. A series of low housing terraces of 1984 fronting a long footpath. Very handsome, with a strong urban quality.

32. Broadwater. This is the remaining part of the old Arsenal canal, constructed 1812-16; the rest of the canal was filled in before the last war. A wide slipway leads down from the Broadwaters Centre, and a footpath runs along the east side of the canal to **Broadwater Lock (32A)**, built 1814, which controlled the entrance to the canal. The old lock gates and the swing bridge (of c1876) which carried the Arsenal light railway across the entrance lock can be seen. One gate is open, but the river gate is firmly shut, cutting off the canal and the lock from the higher level of the river.

33. Gallions Lake. A small lake, with a nice setting provided by the promontory of **Gallions Park** which overlooks it. There is a public footpath round the lake, except to the east, where housing is under construction.

The park too is attractive, extending in the west almost as far as the river wall. To the west of the park is Broadwater Lock *(see 32A)*.

34. A lengthy stretch of the **Eastgate wall** of c1870, which marked the east boundary of the Arsenal before its late 19th century expansion, has been preserved and is clearly visible from the main road.

35. Belmarsh Prison, built 1987-91. On either side of the central brick entrance section, the perimeter wall with its overhanging 'beak' extends for over a kilometre.

36. Crown Court, a post-modernist building of 1993. The two wings are set at an oblique angle to the great central entrance, with its glazed canopy. The building is linked to the prison by an underground tunnel.

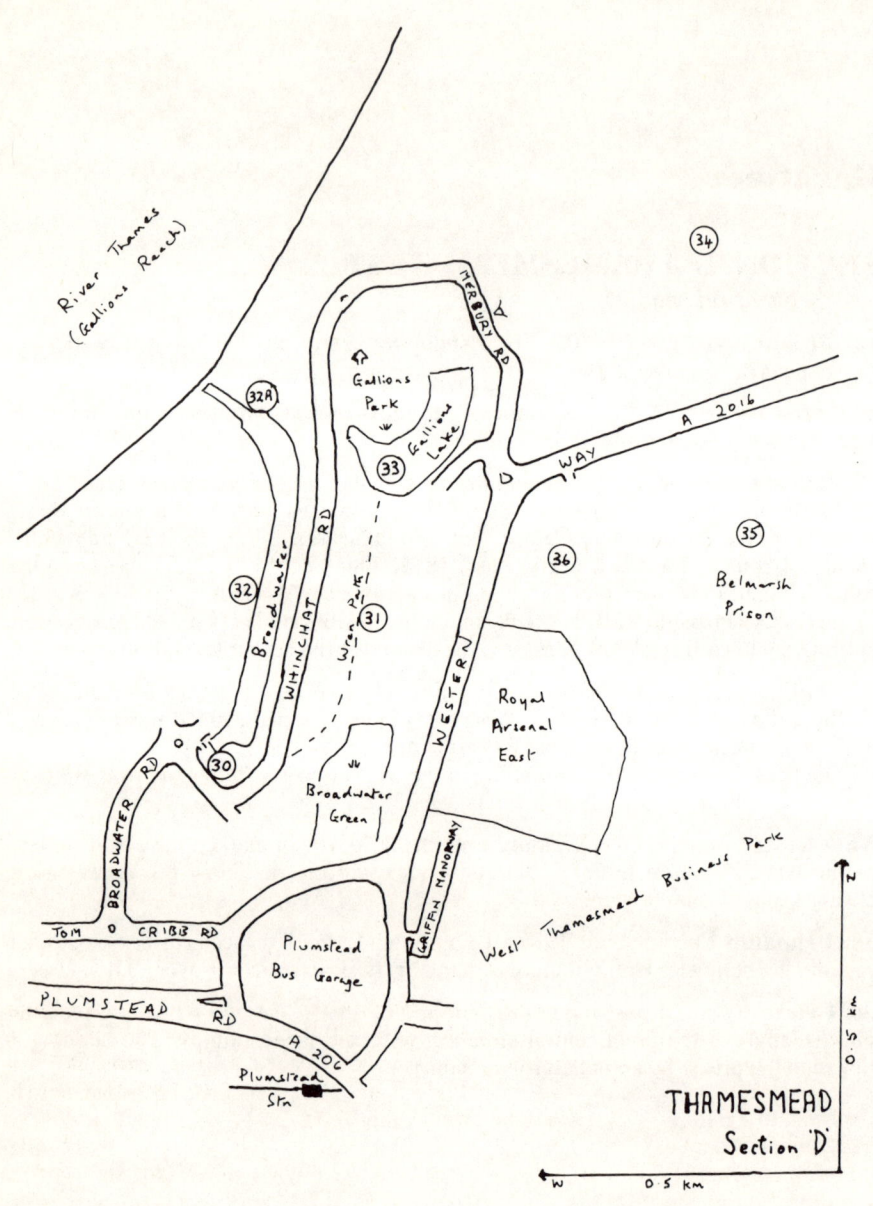

THAMESMEAD

Suggested Walks

These two suggested walks cover Sections 'A' and 'B'. It is recommended that the walks be followed in conjunction with the Gazetteer and the map (on page 80), and that the Gazetteer be consulted at each location. Most locations in these sections described in the Gazetteer are covered.
It is also recommended to walk the full length of the Thameside Walk and back, one way by the high level footpath and the other way by the low level footpath.
There is no suggested walk for Section 'C', as the locations are spread over a large area. However, a walk round Southmere and along Abbey Way is certainly worthwhile. Section 'D' is also not covered, as the locations are few in number and mostly quite near each other, so there is no need to set out a suggested route.
Walk No 1 begins at the Shopping Centre and ends at The Moorings Centre. Walk No 2 follows on, beginning at The Moorings Centre and ending at the Boiler House.

WALK No 1 (Thamesmead Central, including the Shopping Centre, Thamesmere, part of the Thameside Walk, Tump 53). Distance approx three kilometres.
SECTION 'A'. Proceed from the **Clock Tower** away from the **Shopping Centre (1)** to the **Thamesmere Leisure Centre (2A)**. View the **Pumping Station (2B)** from inside the Centre if possible, otherwise from outside the entrance. Proceed down Thamesmere Drive to the roundabout and turn left along Central Way. Take the first road left, following the footpath between high wire fences. Note **Linton Mead School (3)** on the right. Continue until you reach the **Thameside Walk (4)**, then turn left along the high level path.

Continue for some distance, passing Thamesmere and the rear of the Pumping Station, and proceed until you get a good view of the **Thamesmere Extension (4A)**. Retrace steps along the Walk, and turn right down the footpath between high wire fences until you return to Central Way. Cross the road, using the tunnel on the right, to Oriole Way.

Follow Oriole Way to the roundabout, and proceed straight ahead to **Gallions Reach Health Centre (5)**; note the firing range wall behind the car park. Return to the roundabout, then turn right along Bentham Road to **St Pauls Centre (6)**; ask permission to see the interior. Turn right into **Butts Wood (7)** and right again across the canal to **Tump 54 (7A)**. Continue through the woods past the firing range wall to **Waterfield School (8)**.

Return to Butts Wood and take the canal footpath under Bentham Road, then turn right into **Tump 53 (10)**. Return to the footpath, turn right and right again along The Wayleave and continue to the left of the canal until you reach the **Moorings Centre (11)**.

WALK No 2 (Thamesmead North, including Manor Way, part of the Thameside Walk, Crossway Lake). Distance approx four kilometres.
SECTION 'B'. From the Moorings Centre continue east along the canal footpath, passing under Carlyle Road; note the chimneys of the **Boiler House (12)** opposite, and **Moorings Reach (13)** to the left. Bear left along the **Manor Way (14)** footpath which also runs to the left of the canal. Take the footpath left into **Manorway Green (14A)** and **Tump 47**. Retrace steps to Manor Way and cross over to the crescent at the end of **Manor Close (15)**. Continue along the footpath to the left of the canal, cross the bridge, go straight ahead and turn left to **Tump 52 (16)**.

Retrace steps to Manor Way, turn right and continue until you reach the **Thameside Walk (17)**. Turn right along the high level path. Continue, passing the cannon, until you reach **The Cascade (17A)**; if the way ahead is not barred, continue until you can see the beacon at the Crossness headland and the two mid-river platforms, then retrace steps to The Cascade. A short distance beyond, turn left into **Thamesbank Place (18)**, then turn right and left, noting **Drake Crescent (18A)** on the right, until you reach the roundabout.

Cross by the roundabout and go straight ahead into Crossway, turn left into Pointer Close, in the **Lakeview (20)** housing section. Continue to the bridge over Crossway Canal, which provides a good view of **Crossway Lake (19)** and its islands, as well as of **Templar Close (20A)** and the **'square tump' (20B)**.

On the other side of the bridge, turn right down Eastgate Close, then left along Crossway until you reach the roundabout, then left along Summerton Way. Turn right into **Courtland Grove (21)**, then retrace steps. (If you have time, continue along Summerton Way to the **Riverside Golf Course (22)** and the view of Crossness Old Works.) Return along Summerton Way to the roundabout, bear left along Crossway and continue until you reach the Boiler House on the left.

BIBLIOGRAPHY

(including books and publications consulted, and books recommended for further reading, especially for information on local history and architectural detail)

London 2: South, by Bridget Cherry & Nikolaus Pevsner, with section on Bexley by John Newman (Buildings of England series, Penguin Books, 1983)
Handbook to the Environs of London, by James Thorne (1876, republished 1970)
The Industrial Archaeology of South East London (Goldsmiths College Industrial Archaeology Group, 1982)
Charing Cross to Dartford, by Vic Mitchell & Keith Smith (London Suburban Railways, Middleton Press 1990)
Lewisham to Dartford via Bexleyheath and Sidcup, by Vic Mitchell & Keith Smith (London Suburban Railways, Middleton Press 1991)
Greenwich and Dartford Tramways, by Robert Harley (Middleton Press, 1993)
The North Kent Line, by R. W. Kidmer (Oakwood Press, 1977)
The Bexleyheath Line, by Dr Edwin Course (Oakwood Press, 1979)
The Dartford Loop Line, by R. W. Kidmer (Oakwood Press, 1966)
Borough Walks, both old and new series (Bexley Civic Society)
Old Ordnance Survey Maps, published by Alan Godfrey - Belvedere 1895; Bexleyheath North 1895; Barnehurst 1897
A History of Erith, Parts 1-4, by John Prichard (Bexley Libraries 1992)
Belvedere and Bostall, by John Prichard (Bexley Libraries 1994)
The Archaeology of the Bexley Area, by P. J. Tester (Bexley Libraries 1985)
Vickers: A History, by J. D. Scott (1962)
The History of Crayford, by James T. Brown (Crayford Parish Magazine, 1901-08)
The Spot that is called Crayford, by William Carr (Crayford UDC, 1965)
The Industries of Crayford, by J. E. Hamilton (Bexley Libraries 1980)
A Short Account of St Paulinus Church, by Mrs A. Halsall & Mrs J. Bishop (1987)
St John the Baptist Erith, a Church History, by Bob Knight (1994)
A History of All Saints Belvedere, by David Dewsall (1986)
David Evans, The Last of the Old London Textile Printers, by S. D. Chapman (1983)
History of the Textile Processing Industry in the Valley of the River Cray, by Raymond Taylor (1986)
A History of the Slade Green Depot, by Anthony Deller (British Rail, 1994)

All the above publications, and of course many more books, maps and documents, can be consulted at the **Bexley Local Studies Centre**, Hall Place, Bourne Road, Bexley (phone 01322 526574).

INDEX

(Gazetteer references - A = Abbey Wood, B = Belvedere, C = Crayford, E = Erith, S = Slade Green, T = Thamesmead)

Architects, Artists, Engineers
Gordon Allen - C 41, 44; E 39
Sir Joseph Bazalgette - B 34
Binnie & Partners - T 4, 17
Sir Arthur Blomfield & Son - A 7
James Brooks - C 17
Sir Francis Chantrey - E 18
Christiani & Neilsen - B 30
Hugh Easton - C 17
Norman Foster Associates - T 29
William Habershon & Alfred Pite - E 18
William & Edward Habershon - B 19
John Hardman - E 13
C. E. Kempe - E 18
William Mitchell - E 4
Phippen, Randal & Parkes - T 20
James Piers St Aubyn - E 13
Sir Giles Gilbert Scott - T 1
Richard Seifert - E 4, 7
Francis Spear - E 18
Derek Stow - T 5, 25
D. R. Surti - A 14
George Tinworth - E 18
Ward & Hughes - E 13
James Watt & Co - B 34
Sir Bruce White, Wolfe Barry - C 53
Graeme Willson - T 6

Churches etc
All Saints - B 19
Belvedere & Erith Congregational - B 28
Belvedere Methodist - B 5
Christ Church - E 13
Crayford Baptist - C 22
Franciscan Friary - E 28
Free Grace Baptist - B 20D
Jehovahs Witnesses - E 22
Lesnes Abbey - A 1
Our Lady of the Angels - E 28
Queen Street Baptist - E 8
St Andrews - A 12
St Augustines Belvedere - B 9
St Augustines Slade Green - S 8
St Benets - A 8
St Davids Church - A 4B
St John the Baptist - E 18
St Martins - C 34

St Mary of the Crays - C 18
St Michael & All Angels - A 7
St Paulinus - C 17
St Pauls - E 32
St Pauls Ecumenical Centre - T 6
William Temple Church - A 4A

Footpaths
Abbey Way - T 27
Birch Walk - E 24
Cray Riverway - C 42, 52
Manor Way - T 14
May Place - C 36, 37
Riverside Walks - C 52; E 5, 27; B 33; T 4, 17, 22

Housing developments
Abbey Wood Estate - A 4
Barnes Cray Garden Village - C 44
Bostall Estate - A 9
Courtland Grove - T 21
Craymill Estate - C 48
Drake Crescent - T 18A
Greenmead - T 28
Hillside Estate - E 25
Lakeview - T 20
Lesney Park Estate - E 14, 16
Manor Close - T 15
Moorings Reach - T 13
Northumberland Heath Estate - E 39
Pims Almshouses - C 16
Railway Estate - S 4
Mrs Stables Almshouses - C 14
Stone Court - E 6
Templar Drive - T 20A
Thamesbank Place - T 18
Victoria Scott Court - C 49
Whitehill Estate - C 41
Wolsley Close - C 27
Wren Path - T 31

Industrial archaeology
Anchor Bay - E 10B
Barking Creek Barrier - T 4, 17
BICC - B 29, 31, 33; A 13
Bourne Industrial Park - C 26
Cannon (old) - T 1, 17, 24
Chalk mines - A 2, 9A, 19
Coal duty markers - C 3C, 40, 51, 52A

INDEX - 95

Co-op Movement - A 9-11
Crayford Bridge - C 8
Crayford Flour Mill - C 47
Crossness Sewage Works - B 34; T 22A
Dartford Creek Barrier - C 53
David Evans works - C 26
Doultons - E 25; B 33
Easton & Anderson - E 9, 10
Erith Deep Wharf - E 9
Erith Oil Works - B 29, 30, 33
Europa Industrial Estate - E 23
Farms & barns - C 43, S 5A
Fraser & Chalmers - E 23, 27
Gas Works - C 20; E 27; B 2
Herbert Clarke - E 7A, 10
Lyles Mineral Water works - C 28
Man-hole - E 26
Observatory - C 37
Plant Construction plc - T 29
Power Stations - C 52; E 4; B 32; T 17, 22
Quarries & landfill - C 2, 3, 52; E 23, 24
Railway bridges & viaducts - C 36, 42, 50
Railway Depot & Estate - S 2, 4
Rail sidings - C 42; S 1; E 10, 17A, 26; B 29
Railway Stations - C 1,31; S 1; E 1; B 1; A 3
Rich Industrial Estate - C 7
Riverside walks, jetties and wharves - C 52; E 5, 9, 10, 27; B 33; T 4, 17, 22, 32A
Royal Arsenal - T 5, 8, 32, 34 (see also Tumps)
Sewage - C 6, 42; B 34; T 4, 17, 22A
Shopping Centres - E 7; T 1
Textile printing - C 7A, 19, 26, 42
Thamesmead Boiler House - T 12
Thamesmere Pumping Station - T 2B, 4
Tumps - C 52; T 7A, 10, 15A, 16, 19A, 20B
Vickers / Maxim - C 4, 5, 7, 8, 41, 42, 44; E 17A, 20, 21, 23, 26, 27, 39; B 29
Water works - C 3E, 30A
Windmill base - E 33

Leisure
Barnehurst Golf Course - C 36
Cinemas (former) - C 8A; E 6, 7A, 22
Crayford Greyhound Stadium - C 29
Erith Playhouse - E 6
Erith Yacht Club - E 11
Geoffrey Whitworth Theatre - C 44A
Riverside Golf Course - T 22
Riverside Swimming Centre - E 4
Thamesmere Leisure Centre - T 2A

Listed buildings - Grade 1, II* & Ancient Monuments
Crossness Beam Engine House - B 34A
Howbury moated site - S 5B
Lesnes Abbey ruins - A 1
St John the Baptist Church - E 18
St Paulinus Church - C 17

Parks, woods, open spaces
Belvedere Green - B 23
Birchmere Park - T 9
Bostall Heath - A 11
Bostall Woods - A 19
Bursted Wood - C 33
Butts Wood - T 7
Clam Field - A 11
Crayford Stadium Rough - C 30
Crossway Park - T 23
Erith Cemetery - E 29
Frank's Park - B 10
Gallions Park - T 33
Holly Hill - B 15
Hurst Woods - A 2
Lesnes Abbey Woods - A 2
Manorway Green - T 14A
Martens Grove - C 39
Plumstead Cemetery - A 22
Riverside Gardens - E 5
Shenstone Park - C 19
Southmere Park - T 26
Stream Way - B 21

People
Augustus Applegath - C 18, 19, 26, 42
Barne family - C 17, 36, 37
Frank Beadle - B 10, 14
Algernon Blackwood - C 8, 37
Sir Tom Callender - B 21; A 13
Sir Alfred Clapham - A 1
Richard de Lucy - E 4; A 1
Draper family - C 17, 36; S 5
Eardley family - E 18; B 11, 19, 35
F. C. Elliston-Erwood - A 1
David Evans - C 17, 19, 26
Shovel family - C 17, 36; S 5
Countess of Shrewsbury - E 4, 18
Flaxman Spurrell - C 49; B 26
Charles Swaisland - C 7, 14, 26, 42
Francis Vanacker - E 18
Wheatley Family - E 12, 14, 18, 23

Public buildings (present & former)
Belmarsh Prison - T 35
Crayford Town Hall - C 4
Crown Court - T 36
Erith Hospital - E 15
Erith Library & Museum - E 3
Erith Police Station - E 6
Erith Town Hall - E 2
Gallions Reach Health Centre - T 5
Greenwich & Bexley Hospice - A 11B
Lakeside Health Centre - T 25

Pubs
Abbey Arms - A 5
Bear & Ragged Staff - C 9
Belvedere - B 3

Brewers Arms - E 37
Crayford Arms - C 11
Cross Keys - E 6
Duchess of Kent - E 30
Duke of Northumberland - E 38
Duke of Wellington - C 25
Eardley Arms - B 25
Fox - B 20
Harrow Inn - A 6
Lord Raglan - S 6
Jolly Farmers - C 46
Nordenfeldt - E 21
Old Leather Bottle - B 8
One Bell - C 13
Prince Alfred - B 7A
Queens Head - B 20E
Railway Tavern - S 3
Red Barn - C 32
Royal Alfred - E 10A
Royal Charlotte - C 3A
Running Horses - E 5
Trafalgar - E 17B
Wat Tyler - T 1
White Hart - E 6

Schools & colleges
Alexander McLeod School - A 10
Bexley College - B 13, 16; A 16
Crayford Manor House - C 37
Erith Road Campus - B 16
Linton Mead School - T 3
Northumberland Heath School - E 31
St Josephs Campus - A 16
St Josephs School - C 18
St Paulinus School - C 15
St Pauls School - A 21
Slade Green School - S 7
Trinity School - B 14
Waterfield School - T 8

Streets
Abbey Crescent - B 7
Abbey Grove - A 8
Abbey Wood Road - A 7
Avenue Road - E 7A, 12
Barnehurst Avenue - E 39
Barnehurst Road - C 31, 32
Barnes Cray Road - C 44
Bedonwell Road - B 22
Bedwell Road - B 20A
Beech Walk - C 44
Belmont Road - E 35, 36
Bentham Road - T 5-8, 10, 11
Berkhampstead Road - B 27
Bexley Lane - C 22-24
Bexley Road Erith - E 16, 28
Bostall Lane - A 9B, 10
Bourne Road - C 8B, 26
Brampton Road - A 12
Brook Street - E 29-31, 37

Cedar Road - S 4
Chapel Hill - C 21
Cheshunt Road - B 20B
Church Manorway - B 29-31
Corinthian Manorway - E 26; B 33
Crabtree Manorway - B 31, 33
Crayford High Street - C 10-12
Crayford Road - C 4-7, 40, 41
Crayford Way - C 44
Elm Road - S 4
Erith High Street - E 6, 7
Erith Road Barnehurst - C 33, 34
Erith Road Belvedere - B 14, 16-19
Eynsham Drive - A 4
Federation Road - A 9A
Fraser Road - E 22-24
Fremantle Road - B 12
Halt Robin Road - B 6
Harrow Manorway - T 24
Hazel Road - S 4, 6
Hillcrest Road - C 3D
Iron Mill Lane - C 14-16, 45
Lesney Park - E 14
Lesney Park Road - E 14
London Road - C 20, 25, 26A, 28
Lower Park Road - B 3, 4
Maiden Lane - C 40-44
Manor Road - E 10
Mayplace Road East - C 35-37
Mill Road - E 32-34
Milton Road - B 7
Moat Lane - S 4, 5
Norman Road - B 32, 33
Nuxley Road - B 20
Oak Road - S 4
Oakwood Drive - C 38
Old Road - C 13, 18
Orchard Hill - C 21
Park Crescent - E 14, 15
Pembroke Road - E 19, 25
Picardy Road - B 3-5, 26, 28
Pier Road - E 7A
Queen Street - E 8
Sandcliff Road - E 20
Slade Green Road - S 7, 8
Stapley Road - B 20C
Star Hill - C 21
Station Road Crayford - C 3
Thames Road - C 46, 47, 50
Tower Road - B 13
Victoria Road - E 13, 14
Village Green Road - C 44
West Street - E 17
Whitehill Road - C 41
Walnut Tree Road - E 3, 4
West Heath Road - A 17, 18
Wickham Lane - A 21, 22
Willow Road - S 4
Woolwich Road - B 23-25; A 13-16